Ten New Lives
Swedes in the Pacific Northwest

Books & translations by Lars Nordström

IN ENGLISH

The Procession of Memories: Selected Poems 1929 – 1945,
by Harry Martinson (2009)

Swedish Oregon (2008)

Views from a Tuft of Grass, essays by Harry Martinson (2005)
(translated with Erland Anderson)

Seven Kinds of Water (written with Harald Gaski) (2004)

The Road from Rome (1999)

Making It Home (1997)

The Sun, My Father, poems by Nils-Aslak Valkeapää (1997)
(translated with Ralph Salisbury and Harald Gaski)

Trekways of the Wind, poems by Nils-Aslak Valkeapää (1994)
(translated with Ralph Salisbury and Harald Gaski)

Sweden (with Chad Ehlers) (1990)

Between Darkness and Darkness:
Selected Poems by Rolf Aggestam (1989)
(translated with Erland Anderson)

IN SWEDISH

De nya utvandrarna: Tio svenskar i nordvästra USA berättar (2005)

Sju slags vatten (written with Harald Gaski) (2004)

Där du alltid är (2003)

Rapport från en avlägsen plats (poems by William Stafford) (2003)

Min vingård i Oregon (1999)

Ten New Lives
Swedes in the Pacific Northwest

Lars Nordström

SWEDISH ROOTS IN OREGON PRESS
PORTLAND, OREGON

Acknowledgements

This book was originally published in Sweden in 2005 as *De nya utvandrarna: Tio svenskar i nordvästra USA berättar*. The author would like to thank his Swedish publisher, Magnus Ringgren and Edition Edda, for his support of this book.

English translation Copyright © Lars Nordström.

The translator would like to thank Cynthia Nordström for her help with the initial drafts, and for coming up with the title; George Venn for his professional editing of the manuscript. His keen observations, thoughtful commentary, and helpful suggestions improved this book tremendously. Thanks also to Barry Peterson for proofreading the manuscript. To all of you: *Tusen tack!*

In addition, the translator would like to thank Erland Anderson and Ingrid Cassady for their generous help in assisting with the translation of *Carin's* story.

And last but not least, the author wants to thank all the story-tellers for their on-going participation and willingness to answer questions.

This publication was made possible, in part, by a generous donation from Barbro Osher Pro Suecia Foundation and with financial support from Swedish Society Linnea.

Swedish Roots in Oregon Press
8740 SW Oleson Rd
Portland, OR 97223
swedishrootsinoregon.org

Lars Nordström, larsnordstrom.com

First edition

ISBN 978-1-4507-4928-2

Printed in the United States of America.

Book design by Kristin Summers, redbatdesign.com
Cover design and photography by Lubosh Cech, OkoDesignStudio.com

TABLE OF CONTENTS

INTRODUCTION

In 1997, after having lived in Oregon for about fifteen years, I published a book entitled *Making It Home.* It started out as an attempt to portray a year on the Oregon farm on which I lived, but it also grew into a memoir when I discovered that my Swedish past was inextricably intertwined with my new life in America. I was an immigrant in the post-Vietnam War period, and my own fate was, I thought, just a strange combination of serendipity and circumstance. I knew I was an atypical immigrant, having become a grape grower on the one hand, and a translator and author on the other. Reading from the book in front of audiences, and trying to answer all kinds of questions about it, made me increasingly curious about other Swedish immigrants. I certainly knew my own story, but why had the others come? What did a typical Swedish immigrant of my generation look like? What kept them here? I just did not know.

To learn more about Swedish immigration to the Pacific Northwest, I started to do some research. I discovered that Ernst Skarstedt had written several books on this subject, as had Svante Löfgren, but they described Swedes from that first wave of immigrants well over a hundred years ago. I also found a charming collection of oral histories in English entitled *New Land, New Lives: Scandinavian Immigrants to the Pacific Northwest*. It contained 45 short narratives by Scandinavians who had immigrated to the Pacific Northwest between 1900 and 1939. Their stories were exactly what my grandmother and grandfather would have experienced if they had decided to emigrate. All these books were interesting reading, but it was obvious that they spoke of an entirely different reality from the one I had experienced myself. The Sweden these people had left was not the country I had grown up in, and the America they described was not the United States I had encountered.

I kept searching, but could not find a single book that depicted the life of Swedes in the United States during the last 25 – 30 years. There were some articles in the Swedish and Swedish-American press, but these individuals had come for very different reasons. They were primarily sports stars, businessmen, entrepreneurs, and international celebrities enticed by "the land of opportunity," and that they had found their way to the United States was not that surprising. But those were not the Swedes I had ever run across myself; the ones I had met were integrated into American society, lived in the suburbs like everyone else, had American friends, commuted to work, and had children in the local school system.

What I was curious about was this: Why did Swedes of my generation choose to leave a country which for the most part provided its citizens with social justice, a decent education, employment, generous benefits and vacations, as well as a single-payer, universal health care system? In order to find out, during a four-year period from 1998 to

2001, I interviewed Swedes who had settled in the Pacific Northwest following the Vietnam War and asked them to tell their stories and describe the road that had led them here. The interviews were then transformed into the narratives of this book.

Who are the narrators of these stories? I did not try to locate individuals belonging to a specific class or a particular type of profession, and I did not want to influence or steer the selection process. Instead, I simply started asking people in my circle of friends and acquaintances and let the rings widen and grow. Ultimately, serendipity determined the process. Some immigrants I knew quite well and others I had just said hello to at some of the Swedish community gatherings occasionally arranged in Oregon. Many who were asked to participate declined, and not all the recorded interviews were included in this book.

My selection criteria were minimal. The participants should have lived in the United States for at least ten years to be really settled here, and I wanted to balance the participants equally between men and women to make sure that any gender differences would be covered. At the time of the interviews, most participants were in their 40s, married, and with children living at home. Only Tobbe had become a US citizen. All the other participants were Swedish citizens living in the United States as permanent, resident aliens—except Maria, who had been one too, before she moved back to Sweden.

To make our conversation easier, I had assembled four pages of questions that all the interviewees had a week to think about before we sat down to talk. Using these questions as a starting point, they were free to describe the path that led to their present life. I also asked them to reflect on identity, cultural differences, their relationship to Sweden, their bilingual efforts (especially as far as their children were concerned), new insights and perspectives, drawbacks and advantages, as well as their plans for the future. Our conversations—with one exception—were held in the participant's home, and usually lasted three to four hours. We always spoke Swedish.

People do not speak the way they write, and not everyone is a born storyteller—but someone might still be a keen observer and have interesting things to say. Spoken language is full of repetitions; sentences that are never completed; unclear clauses, pronouns, and references; unfinished comparisons; sudden additions; changes in tense; as well as minor grammatical mistakes which one rarely sees in print. In short, a conversation that is transcribed word for word is rarely very easy or interesting to read. For this reason, the transcriptions were edited for readability, and this work might best be described as walking a tightrope—always striving to balance fluency with coherence, and content with the individual voice.

In some instances almost half of the original conversation was cut, passages were moved around for the sake of unity, and the questions were eliminated so that the dialogue was transformed into an autobiographical narrative. Following my editorial work on the text, some participants chose not to touch the text at all, whereas others combed through their stories once or even twice, something an observant reader might notice. All the interviewees have, in other words, always been provided the opportunity to get the last word in their stories, and the end result is always the narrator's own story, not mine. Finally, the English text is a translation of the finalized Swedish narratives, and not the result of additional or later conversations. (I have, however, added a brief Postscript at the end of the book to provide a glimpse of where the narrators are today.)

So what are the reasons for leaving one's homeland? There does not seem to be an easy or simple answer to that question, even though falling in love with an American often seems to be a significant reason. For most modern emigrants the very word "emigrate" seems too definitive. Few feel like emigrants in the traditional sense, but are much more at ease thinking of themselves as "Swedes living abroad." These "expat" Swedes have indeed left Sweden and have become permanent residents of the United States, and they have no specific plans for moving back. In some cases, they have just "ended up" in America following their spouse; they live here "for the time being;" they have decided to "wait and see." Just as the earlier emigrants of a hundred years ago, the new emigrants talk of "going home" when they visit Sweden, even though they obviously have both settled and developed family ties in their new homeland.

The reasons these Swedes still remain abroad vary. The majority live in mixed marriages, and according to some of these oral histories, the narrators' American spouses do not seem eager to settle in Sweden. Reading between the lines, other reasons emerge: the interviewees enjoy their life in the United States; their quality of life is high; and they often feel happier and more open in their new country. Finally, the children obviously play a central role— they grow up as Swedish-Americans, shaped primarily by American values, culture, and language. For them, it is natural to continue their education and life in the United

States rather than in Sweden, and that holds their Swedish parent(s) here as well.

My intent has not been to try to prove or discredit one thing or another, or to make a certain argument, but simply to try—as openly and fully as possible—to illuminate the modern Swedish immigrant experience in the United States. In a time when an increasing number of people create new lives for themselves in foreign cultures, it is my hope that these oral histories can provide a better understanding of what it means to be an immigrant in a foreign culture—wherever one comes from, and wherever one settles down.

Lars Nordström,
Beavercreek, November 2010

A Few Immigration Statistics

- From 1850 to 1928, approximately 1.2 million Swedes—20% of the entire population—left their native country. The vast majority came to the United States. Of these, about 200,000 to 300,000 returned home.

- After World War II, the annual immigration to the United States from Sweden has averaged 1,500 to 2,000 individuals.

- Since 1970, the number of Swedish-born in the United States has declined by more than 60 percent and has now slipped under the 50,000 mark.

- Today—according to the US Census—there are more than four million Swedish-Americans in the United States, of whom less than one percent speak Swedish.

- An estimated 300,000 and 400,000 Swedes—out of a total population of 9 million—live outside their native country today.

- Since 1970, Norway has been the number one destination for Swedish emigrants. Today there are approximately 72,000 Swedes in Norway. Many have also moved to other Nordic countries.

- When Sweden joined the European Union in 1995, emigration patterns changed primarily to countries within the EU, especially to the UK, Spain (snowbird destination), Germany, and Belgium.

- Fairly large numbers of Swedes have also settled in Canada, Asia, and Australia.

- According to Swedish census records, the majority of Swedish emigrants (whose parents were both born in Sweden), end up moving back to Sweden.

I

I Had This Feeling
That I Just Had to Travel

Roger (b. 1955)

Beaverton, Oregon, 1998

I really wanted to leave Sweden; I wanted to see the world. Sweden was too small; everything was too confined. Eskilstuna, my home town, was a backwater .... I wanted to get out of there. Anywhere would basically do. But the US was high up on my list, mostly because everything came from there—music, movies .... The Great Country in the West.

When I was a student, there was a huge demand for manpower in Australia. In the 60s people were paid to go there; they imported people, enticed them to come. I was so focused on leaving that I contacted the Australian embassy, and they said that their need was not as great anymore. But I was an electrical engineer, and for that category there was still some demand. They told me that there were four different locations one could choose from, where employers would come and interview. They would pay for my ticket if I committed to a certain period of time. I was ready to do it, so I filled in the forms and had them notarized.

Meanwhile I went to an employment office to see what one could do to get out of Sweden, and learned that there were several Swedish shipping companies looking for ship's electricians. So I gave them my name as well. Then I promptly forgot that and focused entirely on Australia. I did not give the sea any thought at all. But then, like a thunderbolt from the blue, while I was waiting to hear from the Australian embassy, I received a phone call from the Johnson Line in Stockholm asking if I was willing to sign on.

"I don't know," I said, "I have to think about it. This came as a bit of a surprise." Then I remember that she said:

"There's no time to think about it, because you have to leave tomorrow."

"Well, in that case I'm afraid I have to say no," I replied, "because I have a job and I'm supposed to give two weeks notice."

"You're making a big mistake if you don't take this opportunity," she said.

"No, calling in the afternoon and asking me to leave the next morning is just too short a notice," I replied. But then she called back one more time and said:

"I thought that I'd call one more time, because you only get this kind of opportunity once."

"Alright," I said, "I'll go." Then I went to my employer and told him: "I have to quit. I'm taking the train to Norway tomorrow to sign onto a boat." This was perhaps the most important—and greatest—step I have ever taken in my life. It was really good for me. I was 18 years old. It was 1973.

I worked as an electrician on the Johnson Line ships and traveled around to South and North America, and that's when I came to Oregon the first time. I was gone for two years; it was like an ordinary job. You lived on the ship, of course, but in those days the ships were loaded and unloaded differently than they are today. Now the ships arrive at six o'clock in the morning and leave again at three in the afternoon, and during these hours in port, the crew is so busy that they don't have time to go ashore. That's not the way it was then. The ships were break bulk cargo ships and could remain in port for two weeks, and when the weekend came you could go ashore Friday afternoon and return on Monday—if you had a place to stay. So I got to see both Portland and Seattle.

Then I returned home and completed my studies. When I attended school, headhunters came from the multinational giant ASEA,* and we were invited to ASEA headquarters in Västerås. At that time I still had this feeling that I just had to travel. "Well, in that case you should talk to that guy. He will tell you," they said and pointed to one of the men there. This guy told me: "We have 22 employees. We have one here and another one there. Everyone is off somewhere."

This sounded exciting, so I signed on with him. That is how I started working for ASEA. My very first assignment involved going to Iraq. The job I had was called "Start-up Engineer." What they did was basically send us to a plant to get it up and running; everything had to be adjusted

---

* ASEA, *Allmänna Svenska Elektriska AB* [General Swedish Electrical, Inc.] was as an international company from 1883 – 1987. Its focus was on products and systems for generating, transmitting and using electricity. In 1988 it merged with the Swiss company Brown Boveri and is now known as ABB, Ltd.

and tested. I came to the office, sat down, received material for review, and two days later I was on the plane to Iraq. Just me, in the middle of the war raging with Iran. It is different now. Today they send you with someone who is experienced, but in those days the head of that division of engineers was a man from Skåne in southern Sweden. He was of the old school and had this philosophy: "Hire them, throw them in the sea, and those who swim back we keep. Those who sink we have no use for." That was their approach, and turnover was pretty high initially.

After that, I went east and west, north and south. I went everywhere. It is easier to list the countries where I have not been than the ones I have visited. Sometimes I spent two weeks in Korea, three weeks in Australia, and four weeks in South Africa. When I got used to this, I often wished that I could go home when I was out traveling, and when I was home, I wished that I could go out traveling. I looked forward to coming home, and when I got home, I looked forward to leaving. So in a certain sense I always had something to look forward to. I was a bachelor then and had no one but myself to worry about.

I met my wife after I had finished my studies. Eventually we started living together in Eskilstuna, but I had my job in Västerås. I did not spend much time in my office; it was when I came home between trips that I spent time at my office. Then my son was born. He was born in Sweden. During some of my trips—whenever possible—my family came with me. They came to Singapore and Holland. That worked just fine until the children reached school age.

Before our daughter was born we had a big job in a paper mill in Texarkana, Texas. This was a huge project and very important to ASEA in their effort to get into the American paper industry. I got involved in this project from the very start. In Västerås we worked for a long time testing everything before we shipped it to the US. There were six or seven Swedes who stayed in Texarkana for the first two months. I stayed on with my family for another year. It was easy to make friends. The children had a lot to do with it. My son started in daycare. Most of the friends we made, outside of work, were the parents of our children's friends. It was a very positive experience. Everybody got on well. My wife thought that it was exciting to be there, and it was in Texarkana that she acquired a taste for living abroad. I spoke "school English," but now I had to learn their southern dialect. Initially I had problems understanding their accent, and had to ask people to repeat what they had said. This took a month; then I got into it.

It is easier to make new friends in the US than in Sweden, but the acquaintances you have in the US you don't know as well as those you know in Sweden. I have thought a lot about this. I think there are cultural reasons for it, two main reasons. First of all, in Sweden you never move. It is not that way any more perhaps, but that's the way it was twenty years ago. You stay where you were born, and most people remain in their native city. When you get your own place, you basically become a neighbor of your parents. And your parents stay in the place they moved into when they were young, and live there until they die. If you have bought a house in Sweden—and most people only do that once—then you stay in it. It is uncommon to move from one house to another, or to move from Skåne in southern Sweden to Stockholm.

Secondly, the school you attend: from first grade, most of those kids are neighbors and friends, and you go to the same school for seven, eight, nine or ten years, sometimes even longer. So it is the same kind of people. You have known most of your old friends since you were four years old, and you have seen them more or less daily. With friends like that it is very hard for a person from the outside to enter in and have the same feeling of fellowship as the others have. You never get to know them as well as those you have grown up with.

This is very different from the US where they make sure that they move the children around after every grade on purpose. And they start in grade school. So even if you stay in the same school, you get new class mates. On top of that it is very common for people to move. And last, but not least, when you graduate from high school and get ready to go to college, you definitely disappear from your parents and friends. Your friends are scattered and you are forced to make new ones. And everyone comes to the university on the same premise: almost no one has an old childhood friend there. They are all new.

As a result, it is very easy to meet new people in the US, which is the opposite of Sweden. There, people are somewhat reserved and suspicious and wonder who this new fellow might be. I have experienced this many times in airports while traveling in Europe. If you hear some Americans sitting somewhere talking and you walk up to them and ask:

"Are you from the US?"

"Yes," they answer, "what about you?"

"No, but I live there." Then you *are* an American and sit down and drink a beer or something, and talk about everything. Three or four people who have never met each other before! Not so with Swedes: once in Spain I over-heard five or six Swedes talking about golf.

"Oh, you are Swedish!" I said in Swedish.

"Yes," they answered.

"Do you play golf?" But they turned their backs to me and continued talking. I was never allowed into their conversation. I have experienced this many times. Especially when you are out traveling, you can run into a completely unknown American and talk with him about everything. With a Swede you don't know, you immediately hit a wall: "Who the hell are you? And why are you talking to me? I don't know you at all!" There is a difference. But if you somehow manage to get to know that Swede, you will probably have a more durable friendship than that with an American.

There might be two sides to this. The first is probably a kind of obligation in Sweden: that if you have a commitment to be someone's friend, it comes with certain obligations. OK, we are friends now; I will stand by you and you will stand by me. The other is simply that you will get to know this person so well—after a short time you will probably be introduced to his parents, siblings, and friends. You become more involved. In the US you don't become as involved. If you make a friend here, chances are that he is from Florida, his parents currently live in Hawaii, one sibling lives in California, one in Canada, one in Europe, and you will never get to meet them. And his old friends from school, with whom he played football or baseball: they are not here either. So the only thing you will get to know of him is what he is here and now. You will never get to know him any more than that. Suddenly he will get a new job in Connecticut or some place like that, and off he goes. That's the difference; as human beings you are not different.

During our stay in Texarkana I had a one-year contract. We knew we were going back home. It was exciting, of course. In the beginning, before we knew anyone, we had all these Swedes to socialize with. Because I had my family with me, we lived in a row house, but all the others stayed in hotels. So it was natural that we would gather at our place in the evenings, especially on the weekends, to barbecue. Back home we only barbecued pork loin; in Texarkana we started barbecuing T-bone steaks. Meanwhile my wife had begun to get to know some people, so once the others returned to Sweden, we started to socialize with them. So we were never isolated. We still keep in touch with some people down there. Before returning to Sweden we ended up in Knoxville, Tennessee, for several months, so in all we stayed abroad for a year and a half.

Returning home that time, my view of Sweden had not changed. Among other things, it probably had to do with the fact that I was still employed—on loan from ASEA Sweden. On the other hand I think that both of us, after a while, felt that we did not want to stay in Sweden. We had developed a taste for this. It was not something we decided to do, but we felt the same way. After I returned home, I was assigned to another long job in Holland, and the family came along once again. We stayed there for half a year. Then we returned to Sweden, and my daughter was born. At this point I was supposed to quit traveling, because our son was going to start pre-school. I got a job at ASEA Service in Eskilstuna and became the service manager of a group of engineers there. We settled down in Eskilstuna, bought a row house within bicycling distance to work. I had my office and the guys that worked for me. I was in charge of planning and things like that. That was the way it was supposed to be from now on.

I could only stand that for a while, then I realized that every day was the same. The customers were a little bit different, but the job was too monotonous. I was there for maybe a year and a half, then I started taking some of the jobs myself. I used my old contacts and occasionally asked if they needed help, because I had to go somewhere every now and then. So I started traveling to Spain and Italy, to paper mills that had problems. That's when I ran into this fellow named Sune; I had worked for him in Texarkana. He needed someone in the Pacific Northwest. This was perfect. You don't immediately answer yes or no when someone asks you to emigrate. They would be back in touch once I had given this some thought. I picked up the phone right away and gave my wife a call: "Do you want to move to the Pacific Northwest?" We learned one thing in Texarkana: if we were going to live in the US, we did not really want to live in the South. The cultural differences between the southern US and Sweden are too great. Among other things, it has to do with the churches and religion. It is almost like Sweden and Spain—they are not the same country. In the South, they have the same president, the same dollar, almost the same language, but everything else is completely different. For a Scandinavian, it is much easier to live in the Pacific Northwest than in the South. So my wife's immediate response was: "I sure do!"

At this time ASEA—and many other large international companies—offered their employees work-abroad contracts. These contracts included insurance coverage and a free, annual trip home for the entire family. Not that many employees were offered the chance to go—we all knew that. The jobs were coveted. Many had the opportunity to go to India or Russia, where there were large demands for Swedish engineers, but you can't really move there with a family. The US is one of the few countries where you can think of bringing your family along.

In those days it was common that the contracts ran for two years. Our son had not started school yet, so we had to make a fairly quick decision: we would not go, and he would start in a Swedish school, or we would go and let him start in an American school where he could learn English quickly. We could always return to Sweden to let him continue there, and on those premises we left. And this time our move was a bit more definitive. We sold our row house and packed the contents into a 40 foot container. Everything we owned ended up here. I came over on a scouting trip to check things out. Initially we rented a house. That was in 1989. It was not a huge step because the company paid for everything, had the container unloaded, and the house furnished. It almost looked like it had back home.

Those two years rushed by and we extended the contract one year at a time. Then the times began to change in Sweden and so did the Swedish companies. Initially these companies thought that it was important to have Swedes abroad. The reason for going was that you would train local people to do the work, but it never worked out that way. You had to do everything yourself. So when one Swede left, he took everything with him, so they were forced to send another anyway. During the years I was gone, this began to change. It was expensive to keep a Swede abroad, so they sent fewer and fewer. They began to cut out the fringe benefits from the contracts, and finally, ASEA in Sweden gave me an ultimatum: "Next year you have to decide if you want us to keep your job for you. And if you do, you have to come back home. If you don't, your position will disappear and you will be terminated from ASEA Sweden." I had been in Oregon four years when this happened.

So what were we going to do now? Two years earlier we had almost decided—indirectly—because the rental contract for the house only lasted two years, then we bought a house. You put down additional roots when you do that. So we said—OK, let's stay in the US and see what happens. I can always get a new job with ASEA in Sweden. Now I had basically cut myself loose from ASEA. We got on well here. Our son had been attending school in the US for several years now. He had learned English and our daughter spoke English even though she had not started school yet. And times were definitely bad in Sweden in the 90s; they had almost hit bottom. Highly educated people drove taxis and so on. Taking all these things into consideration, we decided that we would not move back home, at least not then. We decided to wait and see, and we are still doing that. We are still not a definitive case. We will probably still wait and see for another twenty years.

There was an additional reason as well. The special work visa I had was only good for five years. After that you either had to leave the country or get a green card. So now we had bought a house, cut our ties to Sweden, had children in school. Then my employer came to me and said: "OK, if you quit your job in Sweden, we will hire you here, but if you are hired locally, the old contract will no longer be in effect. There will be no more free trips back to Sweden, and your insurance will be an ordinary American insurance policy." At that point I did not have much choice, because I had already quit my job in Sweden. So I got hired locally, my "moon-and-the-stars contract" ended, and I got even more rooted here.

The fifth year was soon over and I would have to leave the country if I did not get a green card. At this point my employer promised to help me with that, pay for everything, but in return I had to sign a two-year contract with him, starting the day I got my green card. If I quit before the contract expired, I would have to pay back his expenses for my visa. Now, the process to get a green card took almost a whole year, which was followed by a two-year contract. We are talking seven years now. During this time we thought that since we had established ourselves here, we wanted a house that we liked a little better. That's when we built our house. That was another root, and when we moved in, both kids were in school. My son is in middle school now, and he has almost forgotten everything about Sweden.

At that point I was employed here, I lived here, I had my green card, and everything had been cut off from Sweden. I had no more business dealings with Sweden. About this time I had been an employee for so long that a thought took hold in my head—it was time to do something else, start working as a consultant. So that is what I did. And then I put down even more roots here, because what I do now I am not sure that I can do in Sweden. Doing this kind of work probably only works in the United States. If we were to move now, we would have to start over in Sweden. I believe that I would be able to get a job in Sweden without any problems, almost anywhere I wanted.

We had a great contract when we moved here. We kept that until we cut our ties with Sweden, but that was a decision *we* made. If we had been uncertain about it, I would never have terminated it. It was never difficult to cut my ties with Sweden.

Those years in Sweden, those long years in Sweden when I paid formidable taxes—they are now to my advantage for my retirement. Nevertheless, I haven't really figured on ever getting anything back from it. So my plan is to support myself on what I can save here. I am not entirely happy with that, because most people start saving for their retirement when they are in their early twenties, but I started when I was almost 40. But I don't intend to retire when I am 60 either. I can't; I have to work. If I continue as a consultant, even as I get older and beyond retirement age, and as long as my health is good, there is nothing that says that I have to quit working. I can take on consulting jobs when I feel like it—if there are any jobs to be had. I think there always will be. Personally I don't believe in working full time my whole life and then suddenly quitting. I don't think I could handle just quitting. In that case I would have to scale down working gradually. This spring I was in Columbia working with some Germans, and there was a fellow there who was 72 years old! He did not want to retire, not yet at least. He did not know what else to do.

Looking far ahead to my retirement, I can't take financial planning alone into consideration. It is also about having something to do. I really like golf, and I could easily play golf every day for the rest of my life. But I don't know if I would feel satisfied doing that. Right now I am saving to see if I will need the money at all. Obviously I think about it: otherwise I would not even bother to save for my retirement. *Will I be able—on the day I turn 62—to provide for myself for another 20 years on my savings? We'll manage somehow; I believe it will work out.*

My opinion about the United States started to change the day I began living here permanently. Once you're in the system, living the American way, and paying for things like retirement, health care, education, and insurance, you see how everything is run and decided by insurance companies and attorneys. I was not really aware of that when I lived here temporarily. That is probably the greatest surprise—that you have personal responsibility for someone who might sprain his ankle in your yard—things like that. This is just the insurance companies trying to rake in as much money as possible and pay out as little as possible. And there is nothing unique about that. All the money left over is then divided between the insurance companies and the attorneys. It makes them rich and is nothing but a nuisance to the rest of us. This is my greatest disappointment, I think. It makes everything very complicated. Without them it would not be so bad. And it is not because I am self-employed; it is something systemic that everyone has to wrestle with on a daily basis. Everything that is complicated and annoying—and this is my personal point of view—can be traced back to attorneys and insurance companies. When you buy a house here, or just re-finance your loan, there are 75 papers that you have to sign. It takes a whole day to sign all the papers. When I asked why there were so many papers to sign, they answered that behind every one was a lawsuit that they were trying to prevent. Who is responsible? Who is not responsible? Who is supposed to pay? Without doubt, this aspect is what is most inconvenient here, and it influences your sense of freedom.

I find education missing in the American schools. It is not that they are just babysitting, but the schools seem poorly structured. The students don't—to be blunt about it—get their rears in gear. They don't learn enough and they spend too much time on unnecessary things. The schools are, simply put, inefficient. I think a main reason is that the schools basically organize their instruction school by school. And many of the teachers—and I am just guessing now—learn a bunch of baloney when they train to become teachers. Psychology. That pampering is part of it; that it should be pedagogical; that a lot of time should be spent doing it. They don't have the right objectives. If you want to reach this level [holds his hand chest high], you have to strive for this [holds his hand above his head], then you will end up where you want to be. But if they want to reach that level, if they have that level as a goal, then they end up here [holds his hand low]. That Swedish exchange students find American schools so easy is explained by the fact that when they come here, they have already studied the same things in the Swedish schools.

Unfortunately, things are sort of like that in general in the United States—that is why it is easy for me to have the job I do. I might not, perhaps, be able to compete as easily back home in Sweden. Many Americans get nothing done. They are busy, they are occupied—fabulously occupied—but after twenty hours they have only come a short distance. They get nothing done, and this begins in school. Long days, no breaks, many more hours in school than what they have in Sweden—and nothing gets done!

It must be very difficult later, when those who are used to never getting anything done enters the US job market, because there the opposite is true. There, it works like this: "This is how it is to be done; this is the objective. If it is not accomplished, everybody gets fired. And we start all over again." People go from school to a working life where business strategies are among the most efficient in the world. What a step! It is a very small group who make it there. They get there through expensive educations. They can't approve or accept anything with a standard that is lower than what they have already set for themselves. For everyone who has not reached that level of education, but still tries to get there, it is very difficult. Of course, there are large numbers of skilled people in the technical fields and in business; those who are good are the world's best. Then there is a gigantic gap to the rest. It is as if competence does not reach all the way down.

I know that there are other things that don't work well in the United States, especially if you have an inferior education and a job that is bad or poorly paid. But I have no personal experience of this. If people don't have any money, things will turn out very badly. That is why you feel so secure here as a Swede, because if things go straight to hell, you can always return. We have an escape route, and those who are born here don't have that.

I don't know that dealing with government agencies and other bureaucracies is that much easier here. My impression is that it is just as troublesome as in Sweden. On the other hand I have forgotten most of what it was like there. Because I have my own company here, I am forced to do a lot of paper work. But it might have been that way in Sweden too; I never tried it there. It is tiresome, but I think it is tiresome wherever you are.

I don't think it is more free here than back home. There are all kinds of nationalities and religions represented in this country, and most of them are perhaps here because they feel more free than they did in their native country. Swedes do not usually come here to experience more freedom; they have other reasons.

The economic possibilities are definitely better in the United States. Taxes are not particularly low here; you can't say that it is a paradise for taxpayers. But the difference in income, compared to a similar job in Sweden, is big enough that one can more easily handle the existing—and substantial!—taxation than you can in Sweden. One shouldn't really use words like "cheaper" or "more expensive;" in this context, one should say "better buying power." I don't think that a person here, working in a gas station, has better buying power compared to someone doing that job in Sweden. So it depends on what you do. I couldn't say that I am bombarded by questions exactly, because I come from Sweden. But it is probably true to say that Americans have a somewhat skewed view of Sweden—they know that girls run around topless in the cities. They know so much about Sweden that I have never heard about. And if they at some point have heard that Sweden is a socialist country, they equate that with communism. If anyone in the South knows anything about Sweden and Scandinavia, it is that all inhabitants are most likely communists as a result of the socialist system. But that is probably not true here in the Pacific Northwest. I don't think that the average American has enough knowledge to even be able to comprehend what Sweden has accomplished. Something they ought to be impressed by is the manufacturing industry Sweden used to have. But they are not, because they simply don't know about it. Americans are badly informed in general about international things. They know very little about things that happen outside the United States.

I don't think it is completely meaningless to be a Swede in America, but it depends on what you do. In my working life I have experienced being Swedish as a positive thing. I have come to the opinion that many see Swedes as a bit more professional than others. Not always, but repeatedly I hear: "OK, now we have a Swede here, so damn it! Let's get this problem solved once and for all." Many times I have been seen as more competent than the average American. That has been very positive. I can't recall that I have ever experienced anything negative about being Swedish. If Americans have any opinions at all about Swedes, it is quality and technology. Quality is strongly associated with

Sweden when it comes to industrial things.

It is possible to characterize Swedes in the US, but they are not all the same; you have to divide them into different groups. There is one group—and this is probably true for all nationalities—that is more nationalistic in the US than they would ever have been in Sweden. Then are those who have moved to the US and hardly want to admit that they have anything to do with Sweden. In other words, there are those who reject Sweden and those who are their complete opposites. Then there are those who maintain a more neutral stance, which is what I think I do. I don't think that those who reject Sweden really believe that deep down; it is just a way to justify that they are still here. They don't want to move because they like it here, but they can't say: "I like Sweden too, but I think that I want to stay here." Then it is easier to say: "No, goddamn it, I never want to see any of that again."

I only have one sister left in Sweden, so my ties are not that strong. My wife, on the other hand, still has both her parents, two sisters, and many cousins there. She has definitely much stronger family ties—in part because her family is bigger—but even if we had had an equal number of relatives, she would probably have stronger ties to her family than I would have to mine. I have cousins in Philadelphia. My uncle immigrated here in the 40s. He was a nuclear physicist and worked at the Benjamin Franklin Institute in Philadelphia. I never met him in the US, but I saw him in Sweden when I was a child. We have visited his children in Philadelphia. They don't speak Swedish. My uncle married a Japanese American, so they grew up speaking English.

We visit each other in the family fairly often. My in-laws, especially my father-in-law, like to travel. So they have been here four times in nine years, and we have visited Sweden more or less every other year. The exception is my sister. She does not like traveling and has only been here once. I keep in touch with a few friends from the years before my emigration, but that diminishes exponentially in proportion to the number of years you have been here. When it comes to friends and acquaintances, contacts have definitely decreased in later years. Friends visiting have been few and far in between. Things are the same when you go back; in between, not much happens.

We always speak Swedish at home, and the children answer in English—very rarely in Swedish. A typical conversation around the dinner table is that my wife and I speak Swedish and the children English. When we visit Sweden it takes about a week, then they start getting into Swedish, and after two weeks they basically speak only Swedish. After that it is Swedish all the time. When we return here they speak Swedish until the first friend comes over—then they switch to English again and after that there is nothing but English. Our daughter was so young when we moved here that she has a hard time expressing herself in Swedish. Our son, on the other hand, is pretty fluent in Swedish. But for both of them it is easier to speak English. Language is one reason why we try to go back as often as possible.

Speaking Swedish is important, but it is enough for me to speak it at home. However, it is fun to meet on special occasions, traditional Swedish events like a crayfish party or a pickled herring and potato dinner. It is enjoyable if you can speak nothing but Swedish. Sometimes it is hard if you gather at a traditional Swedish event and then— purely out of politeness—have to speak English because there are a couple of Americans there. That can be a bit unfortunate. In certain situations I feel that I have a great need to stick to my Swedish. I never actively tried to find other Swedes when I moved here; the contacts I had with Swedes I got through my job. I don't think we had a need to do it; it was just serendipity. I don't belong to any Swedish organizations. In my case it probably has to do with the fact that my wife is very involved in them, so the things we do come as a result of her involvement. My personal opinion is that the importance of a Swedish club would not primarily be about exchanging films or magazines, but simply to get together. The need among the Swedes for such a club depends on where in life you are. We have a teenage son and a daughter who is not yet a teenager, and life continuously revolves around school, soccer, horseback riding, homework, and soccer competitions. On the few days when I have time to do something that is unrelated to their activities, it is enjoyable to just sit down and do nothing. I am not active in the various local Swedish-American organizations either, but I know a little bit about them. They do not satisfy our needs, because they are basically Americans with a Swedish connection. These individuals are often quite old.

I have a certain interest in preserving Swedish traditions—not all traditions, but some. Thanks to my wife we probably preserve most of them. If I had been married to an American I would probably have had very few Swedish traditions in my home. But everything we do on holidays such as Christmas is traditionally Swedish. We don't eat very much Swedish food, but one could ask oneself how much Swedish food is really eaten in Sweden? Well, you can prepare *kåldolmar* [stuffed cabbage rolls] here, but that is not eaten very often in Sweden either. During the ten years we have been gone, Swedish food culture has changed a great deal. If you go to a lunch restaurant and pick the daily special, it may not be a Swedish dish. The things that are truly Swedish, that you don't eat anywhere else—crayfish, pickled herring, *surströmming* [fermented Baltic herring], Janson's Temptation, you can buy all of that here. There are a few things that you can't find—fresh herring for example—and that is one of my absolute favorites. You can't find *blodpudding* [blood sausage] either. Otherwise you can basically find or make everything else. There are certain things in Sweden that you eat to the point of exhaustion—hot dogs in a bun, or hot dogs with mashed potatoes and shrimp salad, I eat so many of those from street vendors when I come home that I get tired of them before I leave. So I don't have any need to eat more than twenty of those every other year when I am in Sweden.

We have Swedish culture in our home, but outside the walls of the house there is not very much of it. That's the way it is. One important factor that determines if one feels at home or not comes from how one's home looks. I think we felt at home from the beginning because of all our furniture and household goods. Even if one does not feel entirely at home in this society, at least one has that feeling at home because one has all the Swedish things here. If I were to compare today with ten years ago, I feel more at home now than I did then. But that could change. For me it is not much different than moving into a new house in Sweden; then you are not at home there.

The reason I have kept my Swedish citizenship is that it is—so to speak—my emergency exit. It irritates me that I cannot vote here in the US, but not enough to give up my Swedish citizenship. If it would be possible to have double citizenship, I would definitely do that.

During the time we've been gone, Sweden has changed

considerably as a result of the economy and the political situation with the European Union. And like Sweden itself, the Swedes have changed. I have discovered something about Swedes that was not entirely unknown to me before, but which have become more and more striking the longer I have been out of the country. It probably has to do with the fact that Sweden is such a small country, but all Swedes do the same things at the same time. There are very few Swedes who are different. If you go back home every other year and look around when you step off the plane at the airport at Arlanda, you know what everybody looks like in Sweden. Everyone wears the same kind of glasses, the same kind of pants with same kind of pockets, and everybody does the same thing. Now everybody goes to Thailand on vacation, and if they have not been, they are planning to go. And everyone plays golf, even those who hated golf and thought that I was a bit odd when we moved ten years ago.

I can imagine—again because of the way Swedes are— that they would not spontaneously look at the success of others with a lot of goodwill. For example, if we were to live here for a few more years, sell off everything and move back to Sweden, we would be able to pay cash for a nice house. I don't think the Swedes would like that. Another reason for not moving back to Sweden is that one's children put down roots here. If you don't not have any children, I think you would move back home, at least if you stay here during your active years. Yes, I think you would move back to Sweden. For me it was a prerequisite: if we were going to move with our children, it had to be to a country where English or Swedish was spoken. Distances have shrunk to such an extent today that moving is not uncommon. There are many people who don't mind moving, whatever culture they have. When people came here in the 1930s, it was a definitive move where you left everything behind. It is no longer definitive. I don't think that it is any worse for a contemporary Swede to emigrate to the United States than it was for a person from northern Sweden to move down to Stockholm in the 1960s.

Then you start thinking like this: what is good about living here is that when you have gotten tired of the rain, you can move within the United States and choose the kind of climate you want. You can't do that within Sweden. Of course, with the European Union, moving within the EU is a new thing you can do. Now there are large Swedish colonies down in southern Spain, in Costa del Sol for example, consisting mostly of retirees. That involves another less pleasant aspect—that you live isolated from the local population. Then you live in a Swedish enclave inside another country. For me—above all—it is important to be able to speak the language where you live. I would not feel at home at all if I could not speak the language. You have to adjust to the new culture as far as you are able.

Things have been so good in Sweden that they can now only move in one direction—things can only get worse. Our generation was spoiled as hell; we've been damned lucky. Everything worked when we grew up. Everything was free. Everything ran like clockwork. While we were still students, they came and tried to recruit us, tried to grab us: "This is where you want to work!" "No, come and work for me!" In Sweden it can't get much better; now things will only get worse. They will soon have the same standard of living as the United States. No one will get anything for free. Everyone will have to fight for it. Here in the US things can't get much worse; things can only get better. Here you have to struggle if you want to make it, and there you will have to struggle if you want to make it.

I don't think that my years in the United States have colored my view of Sweden, but I think I have discovered a few things that I did not think about when I lived in Sweden. The things I took for granted in Sweden are not that obvious here. I am thinking about things like health care, medicine, care of the elderly, and schools. You realize why you paid higher taxes. Sweden has not become a more attractive country to live in, and that is probably a combination of the economic crises, the European Union, and maybe immigration, which has become something of a nuisance in Sweden. People have become very racist in Sweden, more than they have ever been before. If there is something positive that has come from immigration to Sweden, it is the food culture.

I am not planning to move back and I am not planning to stay—I am leaving everything open. I will stay here for the time being.

II

I SWORE I WOULD NEVER
RETURN TO AMERICA
Cecilia (b. 1950)

Gig Harbor, Washington, 1998

My father was an artist and the black sheep in his family. He worked on the passenger liner *M/S Gripsholm*, which went back and forth on the Atlantic between Sweden and the United States. He jumped ship in New York in 1939, stayed for a year, and lived in a boarding house. He attended a commercial art school and worked as a house painter to make ends meet. I think he felt terribly out of place the whole time he was in New York, and after a year he had had enough. But what he always talked about, as I grew up, was how fantastic and wonderful the United States was! He subscribed to the *Saturday Evening Post* and *National Geographic*. So he had romantic notions about America in spite of his negative experiences the year he was there.

My mother always dreamed about going abroad to see

the world, but she was stopped by her mother who needed her help. There were four daughters, but my mother was the one who was supposed to stay at home and help out. Daughter Number One went to Stockholm and became a nurse. Number Two married money and became a princess and walked around town wearing gloves and a hat and looking splendid. Mother was Number Three, and the last one was born several years later, almost like an afterthought. My mother worked in a telegraph office and later became a doctor's secretary at the hospital. She was very good at what she did and was offered a job in Paris. This was right before the war, and my grandmother would not let her go. Then the war came and grandmother said: "Now, aren't you happy that you did not go?" But my mother sulked because she had not been allowed to leave, and she said: "War or no war, I should have been in Paris!" Eventually she got there with my sister and her family, and she came to the United States several times when we lived here. I think my mother was very positive to the idea of going abroad.

I grew up in Sundsvall, so I am from the north of Sweden. The first time I came to the United States was as an exchange student 1966 – 67. I stayed in Flint, Michigan. I came over after 9th grade, before starting in Swedish high school. I was curious about the United States, and I had a good friend who had been to America a few years earlier who said: "Oh, Cecilia, you have to do it!" Her experience had been wonderful. I thought it sounded really fun, and my mother supported it: "It is an opportunity, take it! Go. We will help you. Somehow we'll manage!" However, they did not really have any money for something like this.

So I ended up with a family that had a completely different view of the world—of everything! I met some really terrific people, but the family and I did not have very much in common. I did not know them beforehand, but was placed through the organization "Youth for Understanding," which, I learned later, had received support from the CIA. Life in this family became—in some ways—a caricature of American life: they drove their car everywhere; they ate hamburgers. I was like an exotic bird that they could exhibit whenever they felt like it. Then they would say: "Say something in Swedish!" Eventually they told me: "You have to speak with a more pronounced accent so that people can hear that you are a foreigner." I did already look different, because I was twice as tall as they were. Yes, it was a strange experience, but at the same time it was positive too. I learned to stand on my own and make my own decisions. I kept a diary and it helped a great deal. It was enriching, even though it was not exactly what I had expected or desired.

I encountered a couple of these sexual prejudices directed at blonde Swedish women. But I have had pretty sharp elbows when it comes to those things, and because I am so tall, they probably did not want to tussle with me. When those things happened, I just ignored them. Anyway, I swore that I would never return to America. But then I had not been to the West Coast, and you can swear a great deal when you are 17!

I lived in Sundsvall until 1970, then I moved to Stockholm to attend an art school. It was an introductory school for artistic training, and from there I applied to the textile department at the National School of Arts and Design in Stockholm. I managed to get into something called the Friends of Textile Crafts, and it was just a fantastic place to be. It was located in that park-like part of Stockholm called Djurgården.* On foggy mornings I used to ride my bicycle there. I remember that I often rode my bicycle behind the stable with the king's horses. It was simply wonderful. Right opposite the large outdoor museum Skansen, among the small old houses, there is a small, pink, plaster-covered palace with a tiny yard in front. That is where the organization, Friends of Textile Crafts, is housed. There they make large tapestries for public buildings, and they run a school for weaving and offer classes for teachers of handicrafts. In addition, they have a gallery, and they renovate and create textiles for churches.

Never in my whole life had I worked as hard, and enjoyed myself as much, as when I was there. It was completely phenomenal. I wove rag rugs, I wove towels, upholstery fabric, yes, I even tried lace-making. We accomplished a great deal; I can't even remember everything we did. We had wonderful teachers, among them Edna Martin and Laila Lundell. Laila and I still keep in touch by writing Christmas letters to each other every year. During my time at this place I had various odd jobs to make a little bit of money—I had to pay rent, buy materials, and things like that. I lived with friends in various places—in apartments or in collectives. I worked for the postal service for a while; I worked as a part-time janitor in a school; I worked for "The Booth of Four," which sold crafts made by the blind. Then I worked for "The Workshop," which was run by the city of Stockholm. It was a big operation where people of all ages came to do crafts, and where we worked as instructors. The only things people had to pay for were the materials. It was a fantastic place.

* Actually, an island that was once a royal hunting preserve.

My husband, who is American, came into my life just as The Workshop was moving to a new location on a street called Tunnelgatan. He worked on the same street in a leather workshop where he made bags and belts and things like that—all very nice—together with another American. Later on his friend moved his workshop to the Old Town, but by then my husband no longer worked there. Then he had met me and wanted to do something different with his life. When I met him, I think we spoke mostly English, but he is fluent in Swedish. Sometimes I forget words, and then I have to ask him for help. He also worked as a translator in Sweden.

We emigrated in 1977, even though I had not thought of it as an emigration. We had gotten married the spring before in order to qualify for student housing and student flights. We had lived together since 1974 and did not spend much time thinking about getting married, but we thought those were good reasons. The day we got married, my mother came along. She did not even know that she would serve as a witness; she happened to be in Stockholm visiting us at that time. I said: "Mom, can't you come along with us to City Hall on Kungsholmen? There is something we have to do there for our condo. Then we can go and have lunch afterwards." So she tagged along, and as we walked up the steps to City Hall, we met someone in a wedding dress. If I had known that she had a weak heart, I would not have surprised her like this, but then she asked:

"What exactly are you going to do here?"

"Oh, we are just getting married," I answered. She almost fell down the stairs. Then, as we sat there waiting for our turn, she said:

"But I'm wearing Cecilia's ring today!"

"Do I have a ring?" I asked. [Shows her finger with the ring.] This is my great-grandmother's ring. Her name was Laura and she put her initials on the ring, because her husband went to America when she was pregnant with her fourth or fifth child. He worked in an American mine and was killed. That's the ring I am wearing now. Just as my mother was leaving home to come and visit me, she had taken out a few pieces of jewelry, among them this ring, which she normally did not wear. But she was unable to close the drawer in the jewelry box—it was a bit sticky—and the taxi had come and was waiting outside the front door. So she had simply put the ring on her finger and left the drawer open. Coincidence or not, things like that always happened to my mother.

The immigration was pretty easy; I had no problems. I thought it was a bit silly having to carry X-ray pictures and fill out all these forms where you swear that you are not a prostitute or have syphilis or belong to the Communist Party. We came to Eugene, Oregon, because my husband wanted to finish his doctoral dissertation. He had been a student there before, and basically all that was left for him to do was to write his dissertation. He had tried to finish it in Sweden, both in Stockholm and Uppsala, but they wanted him to start from the beginning and take classes he had already taught. So we figured that we would be in Eugene for two years. Life there was temporary and it was our home, but Sweden was also our home. When we first came, I had brought very few things—a wooden box and a trunk. That was basically all we brought with us. So we thought: *Maybe a couple of years, then we might return to Sweden.* We had no clear idea about this, but I don't think we ever thought that we would stay in America this long!

For us, family life did not change significantly when we moved to the US. We lived pretty much the same way we had earlier in Sweden. We moved into student housing, four family apartments per unit. These were old military barracks and the apartments were fairly run down. I had squeezed my loom into a tiny room and used to sit there and look out the window. I remember one day: first I saw a Japanese family dressed in kimonos walking along bowing to people. Then I saw African children playing with a parasol with dots on it. So the whole world paraded by my little window. It was simply fantastic. My husband did not finish his dissertation in two years; it took an eternity, because he also had to work. So we stayed in Eugene and bought a small house on an unpaved road near the university. There were lots of interesting people in Eugene and one could bike everywhere. I have absolutely no complaints; I really liked it there. We made friends who are still close friends. The atmosphere was very nice and there was a lot of art and crafts and things like that. I taught classes a few times and I taught at the university for six months, as a substitute for the woman who was in charge of the tapestry weaving there. You could talk politics and you could talk about everything with people. You did not have to worry about what you said—not like you do here in suburbia. Where I live now, I have to watch my tongue.

Our son was born in Eugene—it was in 1981. First we got Woffie, our dog, then our son was born shortly after that. My mother came and visited us, and actually lived in a house of her own from the day before he was born until he was seven months old. Some good friends of ours had lent her their house. It was really nice and it was a great deal of fun for her, too. She made many friends who later came to visit her in Sweden. She was good at waving her arms and making herself understood in every possible way when her language skills were insufficient. Once our son was born, it became more and more difficult for her to be so far away from her grandchild. After she had a heart attack, she did not dare to make the trip back again. She often said: "Oh, how I wish that you lived closer." That was difficult. And my son was her first grandchild.

After a couple of years we moved on to Portland, and it was not until then that I started to feel the need for more contact with other Swedes. As my son grew older, I wanted him to hear a bit more Swedish. I have always spoken Swedish to him, from the very beginning, and we have remained bilingual ever since. But only having conversations with a child hardly makes for a rich use of the language. We received many Swedish children's books, but that was still a fairly limited language. I often experience a loss of vocabulary. When I speak with my Swedish woman friend, I often notice that it is easier to throw in some American word in the middle of the sentence instead of trying to recall the Swedish word.

If you speak a second language in this culture I think it is very important that you should try to preserve it. Because I believe that your native language is closest to you, the one where you can most easily express yourself. Even if I stumble because I don't use Swedish every day, all those emotionally charged words are in some way still closer in my own language. I also want to preserve that language, especially since I have a child, because studies have shown that children who grow up speaking two languages have this little "channel" opened in their brains, which makes it easier to learn other foreign languages after that. To be able to give your child not only a second language, but another culture too, is one of the best gifts in the whole world. And it gives you a secret language besides! When you sit on the bus or stand in line at the post office, you sometimes have to keep your fingers crossed that no one else speaks the language you speak. We took my mother to an Egyptian restaurant in Portland once, and the owner spoke Swedish. So you never know.

Once in Portland, I was invited to join the Vasa Order of America,[†] and I was sworn in with the secret password whispered into my ear. And the secret password was the name of the city where the next annual gathering was to be held. It was somewhere in America. The whole thing was so absurd! Everything was so secretive. In this hall that they had, in the middle of each wall there was a huge, grand old chair that looked like a throne carved in wood. That was where we, the newcomers, had to wait, quiet and a little apprehensive, to receive our password and to be sworn in by these old people. I went there one more time. That was when they had a Lucia celebration and everything was just as absurd: Swedish-American children standing there, singing words they did not know, their accent so thick when they sang in Swedish that you could not understand them. They were still very much in love with the idea that they were Swedish; they were proud of it. In the middle of the nonsense I almost felt a kind of tenderness for this, too. So I had no desire to go back there again, even though they pursued me and wanted new blood to keep their organization alive. I was not interested in that. It would be the task

---

† The Vasa Order of America started more than a century ago as a benefit fraternal society for Swedish immigrants in the United States.

of a lifetime to try and get them going.

But sometimes I think: *Will things go this far for us too? Will we do the same with our traditions?* I like some of our traditions and it is not that I follow them rigorously, but perhaps it works so that the further away from them you get, the more you try to cling to the identity you have. I think that if you intend to maintain a tradition, you have to do it right. But it is also true that depending on what part of Sweden you come from, you have slightly different notions about how to do something. For example, when people bring meatballs with mushrooms and gravy to a midsummer party—that's not how it is supposed to be. They should be served with the meat juices only. I like the idea of potlucks in general, but you can't have jello on a Walpurgis Night celebration.‡ That is simply not acceptable. I made a typical Swedish Christmas smorgasbord for all the people who worked for my husband's company. A few of them still insisted on bringing Coca-Cola and cup cakes. I told them:

"This is not a potluck; this is my treat."

"Sure, but I want to drink this," they answered. And then they walked around the table picking at the dishes: "What's this?" They ate all the meatballs; they knew what that was.

When we lived in Portland, I had been involved in organizing regular meetings for a group of younger Swedish women, so when we moved up here to Gig Harbor in Washington, I felt the need to continue with something like that. I got to know several Swedish women in the area

---

‡ Known in Sweden as Valborgsmässoafton, it is always celebrated on April 30th with huge bonfires.

and we meet every so often. I believe there is a SWEA§ group up in Seattle, and some of their energy must be devoted to fundraising. Our Swedish group down here discussed whether we should affiliate with them, but we are not that organized. We are just a few Swedish women who would like to get together every now and then, when we feel like it, and exchange magazines. The problem is that a couple of these women have been in the United States for a pretty long time. They came during the late 1940s or 1950s, and belong to a different generation. They are rather conservative, and they came here for different reasons than those that brought us here. I don't know: we speak two different languages. It has now come to the point that some of us feel that we don't have the energy for this older group, so I think that we will split into two.

Those of us who came here during the last twenty to twenty five years did not feel that we wanted to get away from Sweden. We liked it well enough. So I totally agree with this notion that we have just somehow ended up here, in contrast to earlier immigrants who wanted to get away from Sweden. We also came at the end, or almost at the end, of that period when there were quite a few anti-American sentiments in Sweden. It was dissipating, stuff left over from the Vietnam War. Even my sister thought it was pretty strange that we were going to move to the United States. It took many years before they visited. I think their view of the United States was somewhat negative. I also ran into Swedes who, much later on, thought that it was a bit strange to move over here.

Last weekend I went with a group of women to Car-

§ Swedish Women's Educational Association.

son's Hot Springs, and there was a Dutch woman in the car. She told me that where she lives, in Mount Vernon, they have started something the call BSE, Born Somewhere Else. You have something in common when you come from another country: you are an outsider. Perhaps it is not true that these people walk around thinking like this, but I feel that I do not think the way Americans do. I have a different frame of reference, different things to compare with, a different history. So my girlfriend and I became inspired and thought that we would do this too, because then it would be open to people from all kinds of countries. There are so many different nationalities here! I almost think that an international group would be even more fun than the having a Swedish group, because there it is often very easy to hit your head against the wall and say the same things over and over again. Here I encounter people who have never ventured outside the area, or who have been to Seattle once in their lives and are happy with that. Some people only experience the world through their TV, never anything else. It is fascinating to think that some people can live like that today, and be fully satisfied with it.

I think that those of us who moved here quickly realized that the United States can actually contain a huge amount of very different things simultaneously. Take the Pacific Northwest, for example: I find it a completely different world from the rest of the United States. It is not like Sweden, or at least not like Sweden used to be—very homogeneous. Things have changed a great deal in Sweden, but I remember that, just a few years after moving, someone told me about this girl Carola, a Swedish singer. I did not know who she was. "What? Don't you know who

Carola is?" This has rung a bell in my head every now and then as an example: when something new happens in Sweden, then everybody knows about it right away, but here— well, all kinds of new things can happen. Even if Carola is world famous in Sweden, she is not world famous here.

I work with the same things in the United States that I did before I came here: I weave tapestries. I do commissioned work and I make tapestries for exhibits, and occasionally it is actually possible to sell something privately. I have received three really big commissions. One tapestry went to the hospital Merle West Medical Center in Klamath Falls in southern Oregon, one to the Bonneville Power Administration Headquarters in Portland, and the third went to Washington State University in Vancouver, Washington. Art galleries rarely sell anything. It happens once in a blue moon, but since they often add 50%, the price doubles, and tapestries are expensive to produce in the first place. It takes a lot of time to weave tapestries, but on the other hand they are supposed to last for a thousand years. Usually they are not any more expensive than a painting. You don't set the price on a painting based on how long it took to paint, but when it comes to textile art or tapestries, then everything is supposed to be calculated according to the time it took. That this should be the determining factor is not always right, or that you should base the price on the number of square feet. If people insist on that, I think they should use this approach for oil paintings as well. For example, one square meter of oil painting must be cheaper than the same size tapestry! I also make ink drawings for realtors and other clients. Some are used for advertising, some are purely decorative. I have been involved in that for four or five years, since we moved up to

Washington. Drawings are quick money compared to the income from tapestries.

I certainly don't keep up with all the Swedish traditions, but I try to make things festive around Easter, for example, by putting colored feathers on birch branches. But we don't follow the Christmas traditions as much as if we had lived in Sweden. I light candles, decorate and hang Swedish straw creations on our Christmas tree, and I do like the food. Often, however, we try to alternate a Swedish Christmas with my husband's family tradition. Their Christmas is a mixture of Hanukkah and American Christmas, because my husband does not come from a particularly traditional Jewish family either. His sister also combines her holidays; she is married to an Irish Catholic whose mother is French and father is Irish! So they have a Christmas tree too, and a menorah! This last Christmas my sister was here visiting with her family. We celebrated that with American food—we ate a turkey—so that they would have a chance to experience that. That they would come here and eat Swedish Christmas dishes would not have been quite right.

I don't cook much Swedish food during the week. I cook things like Thai, Italian, Indian, and so on. Maybe once a year I make Jansson's Temptation** or meatballs. But I bake Swedish things. I like desserts and things like blueberry cake, saffron bread. IKEA is not that far away and we buy caviar there, occasionally a jar of pickled herring, powdered vanilla sauce, bars of chocolate .... I have introduced *gravlax*†† to many Americans!

** A well-known potato, onion, anchovy and cream casserole.
†† Raw salmon salt-cured with dill and black pepper. Served thinly sliced.

When I first came to the United States, Americans often asked if Sweden was a socialist country. Back in those days I suppose it was "the Swedish model," that there was national health care and things like it that impressed people a great deal. And just this last weekend we talked to a couple who had been to Sweden and thought that it was very nice, that Stockholm was beautiful. But general interest in Sweden is minimal! I don't think that the average American is aware of its existence. I have never heard people laugh derisively about the situation in Sweden either. If people discuss societies in a state of crisis, they speak about the large countries, about Russia. I don't know if ordinary people are aware that the economy and the Swedish model have broken down either. On the other hand, people do recognize Swedish crafts, Swedish design, Swedish interiors, and so on. I notice that simply because I work with crafts. But otherwise, what is it people say? "Oh, you are Swedish. That is interesting." And then there is not much more than that.

One thing that makes long-time Swedish residents of the US upset, I mean this older generation, is this whole business with immigrants in Sweden. The immigrants who have "ruined Sweden." Another comment that I have also heard is that the language has been ruined. They have a different view of how Sweden used to be. Was Sweden really that idyllic when they left? If it had been, maybe they would not have left? They criticize the changes that are making Sweden more international and interesting, I think. The food culture has definitely improved. I think these views come out of a fear of new things, fear of changes, and of what will happen to the Swedes. I have heard from Swedish friends who recently visited us that you can no longer hoist the Swedish flag on your flagpole because the neo-Nazis have claimed it—that and the runes! I don't know if my view of the United States has changed. The country has become more conservative. We have moved here recently too, and things were different in Oregon from what they are in Washington. In Eugene and Portland there was a more developed sense of the public good. Here people prefer their own little place, preferably far away from others. There is more of a Wild West attitude here. Ideally you should have lots of land around you, and most of all you should be close to the water. Neighbors should not be visible, and having to drive for hours to get to a store does not matter as long as you can live like that. That's the dream. You should not discuss things too much with others, but sort of keep to yourself. If you don't, it is easy to get on the wrong side of a person. I often run across that attitude. Everything is really private. I did not encounter that in Oregon. Like the beaches around Gig Harbor, everything is private and it surprised me. When I came here I thought: *Oh, how wonderful it will be to walk along the shore. I love walking on beaches.* And then one can't do it! Later I learned that you really can, but no one tells you that it is allowed. Just as long as you don't stop, or sit down, or pick up an oyster.

In the middle of everything, you yourself change too. I don't know if I would like to stay here forever or if I will move. It is more like I live for the moment. I don't make any plans, or make lists of the things I intend to accomplish in my life that I then check off. Right now we are here. It is not the same place as the one we were in before, partly because we have moved and now live in an area where almost everyone goes to church. Many have a background in the military, and that is about as far away from what we are as is possible. And to compare this reality to the one we had in Eugene or Portland, well, it is very different. It took me five years to get over the move up here, before I started enjoying living up here. It also had to do with the kind of birds that came into the garden, or what I had planted and what came up in the flowerbeds. Having a woman friend has helped a great deal. We have conversations on the phone almost daily. With her, I can talk about everything. It is not just a question of discussing Sweden, but talking about the things happening here, so that we don't think we have gone crazy. Mentally, it helps us both tremendously. Through her I have also met a lot of interesting people.

What I find lacking here—and now we come back to this feeling of being part of something—is that in Sweden, there is a greater sense of responsibility, a collective responsibility in some way, that we have a responsibility for our fellow human beings. My sense is that this is not as common in Washington. Perhaps it has to do with the fact that we live in an area like this; you don't seek contact with your neighbor unless you want to complain about something. We tried having a neighborhood party and I was the chairperson of the neighborhood association for three years, which almost drove me crazy. I think I became seriously depressed afterwards; it was simply impossible to create a sense of community among the neighbors. Fewer and fewer people participated each year. They had no interest in something like that. This is an area where people move through, even if some have lived here for many years. But they keep to themselves. Right now I have a really good relationship with the neighbor straight across, or more accurately, our entire family has a good relationship with them.

Then there are really wonderful people scattered here and there, but it takes a long time to find them. It was a lot easier when you had kids in school, because you met them when you went there to help out, or when the children played at friends' houses.

My siblings and I don't visit each other that often, but after my mother died my sister and I try to meet at least every other year or so. We went to Sweden three years ago and they came here last Christmas. I have a brother in London who we saw when we went over there, combining London and Sweden in one trip. The way I see it, there will be fewer visits now that my mother won't be there as a magnet, even if we also have other friends and relatives in Sweden. There was a family reunion in Sweden, but neither my brother nor I went to it. My sister did and sent pictures. I have a cousin down in Marin County in California who went over and made a video recording of the reunion. As a result of that, I have actually established contact with a distant relative who went to Michigan last year with his family, and who plans to visit the US in April again.

So far this year I have had visits from both my uncle and a couple of old friends, so it has been busy. Later this summer some other friends might show up as well. In general we have quite a few visitors from all over, and it is hard to say how often that happens. Some years it seems that everyone is traveling around, and other years not many at all. I wish I had started a guest book years ago, and even if people don't write in it, I could at least write down when everyone had been here. Lots of people have been here over the years and sometimes they have stayed for a long time. I think it is a great deal of fun.

I keep in touch with quite a few people from the time

before we moved from Sweden. It is difficult for me to call it an emigration, because it sounds so final, so dramatic—is that Vilhelm Moberg's†† fault? Some friends have sort of fallen by the wayside, and if we haven't written to each other for a while, I don't get an answer when I do write. I don't know what happens. You simply lose touch.

We have started to use the internet to keep in touch with Sweden. I write very slowly on a keyboard, and it is as if I can't think when I sit in front of a computer, as if my brain breaks down and goes blank. But I am getting better at it. I have started writing emails to my sister and a friend in Greece, so things are improving. And we do have the Swedish characters that we can easily use on our computer. Sometimes we use the internet to listen to Swedish radio news and things like that. Early on, when this all started, it was fun to visit the government liquor store site and check their prices! We don't do things like that anymore. But when we had Swedish guests recently, they wanted to listen to the Swedish news, and then we listened to the radio broadcasts every day. My husband is in charge of that, so I look over his shoulder. He spends a lot of time surfing the internet.

Sometimes I call my aunt, an uncle in Järvsö, and sometimes I talk to my sister. Those are the only people I call. Now I don't even call Sweden once a month. Since my sister and I email each other, it is not as important to hear her voice as often. Not that once a month is particularly often. We always have good rapport when we see each other, but you can't say it is intense.

---

†† The author of a very popular fictional tetralogy of Swedish emigrants to America around 1850.

Right now I don't subscribe to any Swedish magazines; it gets so expensive. Sometimes I trade them with friends. I don't belong to any Swedish "book-of-the-month" club either, because there is something coercive about that. I do want to choose books myself. But it might be a good idea .... I found a couple of books by Vilhelm Moberg in Swedish at the local library, because the Friends of the Library sell books which people have donated. I don't read in Swedish all that regularly; occasionally I read through a whole bunch of articles. Perhaps I read a couple of Swedish books a year, and then I read Swedish newspapers every now and then. Lord knows if I read Swedish every week! But I do read a lot of American literature, and I squeeze in the Swedish in between.

Something I notice when I come back "home" to Sweden is how different everything is, how many completely different demands are suddenly put upon you. You have to follow the patterns that they live in—you have to fit into them because that's the way things simply ARE! You cannot question this. To be flexible is not accepted in the same way it is here. Here you can choose to live your life in a completely different way. When I see this, I get the feeling that if I were to live in Sweden, I would be forced into this routine and have to take care of this aunt and that aunt, and have dinner with all these different relatives, and take care of them all. In some way it might be that I am slinking away from it. I almost have guilt feelings because I am not there doing all this. I know that I have two aunts who need help. There are other relatives who could do it, but I don't think they share these guilt feelings. They have all gotten stuck in their routines, and here I sit far away realizing that they need me. I ought to be there, because my mother took care of them and supported them, and now she is no longer there and I am her replacement. In some way I have skipped out, abandoned my responsibility a little bit.

I think of Swedish women my own age: they all have this "Swedish wrinkle" between their eyebrows and they walk around absorbed in everything. Somehow, life is so full of trouble. At times like this, when I am back there, I realize how wonderful it is that I don't have to do all that. You can go there as a guest and everybody loves you right then. It is intense, it is great, and you don't have to deal with all the other stuff.

I think that some of the Swedes in Sweden are the same as they have always been. They complain an awful lot, but then there are those who have always been out traveling, seen the world, and in some way that has become a way of life for them. There are some Swedes who almost have become consumers of the world; they consume global journeys. I don't think this existed in the same way before. There were those who traveled abroad—visiting North Africa was something unusual—but now there are so many people out traveling, and they are going to the most exotic places. It is as if they had this check list ... That is certainly different. And the way Swedes eat has changed. They eat more interesting food nowadays.

Among our friends there I don't notice anything negative about the immigration to Sweden; that is all positive. Some of them are immigrants to Sweden themselves! It is a very international group. I think they are very positive about this and feel that the immigrants have made Sweden more interesting, and when I go there, I think so too. And I think the Swedes have opened up a bit also. When you think about something as simple as going to the post office, these days you might actually meet someone who says hello to you when you get up to the counter. They never did that before. They used to look down at their papers and sort of growl: "Hrrrm, errr, yah?" Now they have taken a class in "How to Charm your Customer" and learned that it is actually possible to say "Hi!" and "Thank you!" and smile a little bit.

On the other hand, not everyone in the US is kind and nice either. I had to get a new green card from the INS and it was not a pleasant experience. You had to stand in line all day and get treated rather badly. Apparently they are trying to improve the situation; there have been many reports about it on National Public Radio. INS definitely needed a class in customer service. But most of the time people in America treat you kindly.

When you live in Sweden, you have the feeling that it is pretty centrally located, and that you sort of are at the center of the world. But when you leave, well, then Sweden hardly exists. It is very rare that I hear any news from Sweden, and then I don't know what happens to my own ideas. It still feels important, because that is the place I come from; it is a part of me, but it is not as important as the Swedes think it is. Sweden as a nation is almost the same way: it is very easy to be in Sweden and say that we are world famous and we are so good. You don't have to go out and verify it. I believe it is a kind of isolation that the Swedes exist in, and perhaps it is true that Americans do not listen to what happens in other countries either. Everyone has more than enough with themselves.

I think it is fair to say that Sweden's economic situation has deteriorated pretty substantially since I moved, and with all the unemployment, the standard of living has gone down as well. I don't think that I could have managed by working the way I have done here, but I would have been forced to have a different job too, something with a steady income. Many of our friends have had a pretty tough time. In that respect Sweden has not improved. But occasionally I think about moving back to Sweden; for a long time we actually talked about doing it. But then we thought perhaps not to Sweden. We feel like strangers, even if it is nice to go there occasionally and see friends and that sort of thing. After all, I still don't feel really at home there. But maybe I would somewhere else in Europe or Scandinavia, perhaps Denmark in that case.

The advantage with the European Union would be, since I am still a Swedish citizen, that I would be able to go over there and, if there were any jobs to be had, work wherever I wanted within Europe—in theory—if it really will work the way they say. What is threatened, I suppose, is the various characteristics of the different countries, the things that make a particular country unique—the language, the food, the music. Will that change over time so that Europe will become like the United States? I don't want that to happen. You want to travel from one country to another and have that feeling of being in a different country. I understand the practical advantages to having the same currency, which they intend to have soon, but at the same time part of the charm is to experience all the variations, all the changes. So my feelings are a bit mixed.

It is difficult to say what I would do if my American husband disappeared from my life. In that case it would depend on where my son was in his life. I am really divided about this. I don't know what would happen. If I felt that

I had more friends in Sweden than here …. Get together with a bunch of friends and get a house in the south of France and live there instead? Many of the things that have happened in my life have—somehow—often fallen into place when they had to. Then I follow that thread instead of saying: "OK, now I will do this." In cases like this I take the train when it arrives.

I am not an American citizen because I am Swedish. I am a Swede. That is my identity. I am not an American. It would be completely incomprehensible if I were to ask an American: "Why don't you become a Chinese citizen?" But it is obvious to me. Sure, I have thought about it—it would be practical and I would be able to vote. But I have a really hard time with the words, and with holding my hand on my heart saying "The Pledge of Allegiance." I am not a nationalist either when it comes to Sweden, claiming that Sweden is best and that is why I am Swedish. All right, I am a European. That's where I come from, but I live here. I would be able to live anywhere and that would be my home. But I don't want to stand there holding my hand on my heart—that just represents a little bit too much of all those terrible things that the United States has supported. I think this has to do with my experience in Flint, Michigan—all those football games and other events when you were supposed to stand like that. Initially I stood with my arms and hands straight down and got all these angry comments all around me to put my hand on my heart, and eventually I stood there with my hand on my heart. But I still did not say anything. It was not my country and I was not going to do it. It was a bit stubborn of me, but I did not even want to pretend that I was an American. And then people looked at me angrily, that I was somehow un-American. Yes, I am un-American! To them it was in some way a slap in the face. It was connected to God and everything. It was ugly.

I did not feel like an emigrant until after my mother died four years ago, and I suddenly had all these things that I had shipped over here after the funeral. You can see that as a sign of not belonging anywhere, or you can see that as a sign of belonging everywhere. And wherever you settle down to live is your home. Right now that is Gig Harbor. But it did not become home for real until my mother had died, and we had sold her condo and the furniture had arrived here. That was the first time I felt: *I suppose I have moved here now.* That's when it hit me. And the trip to Sweden after that was the first time I had gone there and stood on top of Katarinahissen[§§] and not cried because it was so beautiful. That was the first time I felt: *OK, I didn't belong there anymore.* It was very sad. I had cut my ties, for good and for bad. I would really like to have all of that. We still have friends and family there, but it is not the same. When my mother lived in her condo, I returned to our old place; I came to our old apartment; I came to the building where I knew everybody. So it was home. But the last time we visited there, we stayed in one of the other apartments in the building, and that felt strange.

I have thought about this whole thing of being buried in Sweden. Even if I don't think that one should split oneself up—because I would like to be cremated—I think I would like to have some of my ashes placed at the cemetery on Kungsholmen in Stockholm, and some along the Oregon coast. You end up thinking about things like this,

§§ Famous view point in central Stockholm.

especially when you are so far away from home. When we lived in Oregon, I said I would like to have my ashes scattered on the highest peak along the Oregon coast. But now I don't think that I want to have them divided. My mother's ashes are scattered in the memorial grove on Kungsholmen—she had told us what she wanted—and I do like to be able to go to a specific place and not just see a landscape and say: "She is here somewhere!" I suppose I want it to be possible to touch the earth and say: exactly here. I can sit down on a bench and talk to her. I can sit here too and talk to her, but I know there are others who also go there and talk to her in the memorial grove by the church on Kungsholmen.

III

I HAVE PERHAPS BECOME MORE AMERICAN THAN I REALIZE

Jan (b. 1958)

West Linn, Oregon, 2000

What happened was that I did not get the job, the scholarship, or the possibilities I had hoped for. I did get a scholarship to Germany, but said no thanks, and I did not get the job I wanted—even though I thought my chances were pretty good. This was after high school and I lived in Strängnäs. I thought: *What do I do now?* My sister had worked as an *au pair* in England, and I like children—I have five siblings—so taking care of children was something I had done before. This could be a way to go somewhere! So I started looking for *au pair* work. All I really wanted was to experience another country, learn English, and get away for a while—do something different. I wanted to go far away. England was a bit too close to Sweden. I wanted to go either to Australia or the United States. I don't know what it was that made me interested in Australia—perhaps it was the weather, the language, and the life style that seemed fun. I had also always been interested in the United States, especially the West Coast: climate, cars, nature, this and that. There is so much of everything, so much to sink your teeth into. I thought Sweden was pretty small and limited in many ways.

I looked in the two major Swedish newspapers, *Svenska Dagbladet* and *Dagens Nyheter*, and answered quite a few ads. In those days many might have hesitated to hire a young man, but finally someone responded in Lake Tahoe, California. This was in 1979. I believe that I might have been the first male *au pair* in the entire USA, or one of them at least. Later I overheard mothers talking: "What does he do when he changes their diapers? And when he gives her a bath?" As if me seeing the children naked was something strange! I didn't know what they were talking about; I thought it was so weird.

During high school and my military service I worked part-time, and the last thing I remember my employer saying to me was:

"Who knows? Maybe you'll end up living over there!"

That was the morning before I left, and I laughed at him and answered:

"Well, I suppose we'll find out!" But I did not think I would. It was not planned at all. I wanted to go there and not have any regrets later. I heard older people say that they regretted what they had not done. I thought that I would not be the one saying "I wish I had done this." I thought: *No, now I am going to try this. One way or another, I will always get something out of this.* So that was my idea: I would return to Sweden after a year.

I flew to Los Angeles and met a friend from school who

had moved there, and then I met two more friends who were there on vacation. It was summer-like, 82 degrees even though it was December! That was a pretty nice start. Everything was so big—freeways and cars, lots of people. I suppose you can say that there was an abundance of everything. It was fantastic. I was only there for a week before I took the bus up to Lake Tahoe. There was snow there. Squaw Valley had hosted the Winter Olympics in 1960, so it has a winter season. It was fairly populated around the lake, and Truckee, Squaw Valley, Alpine, and Tahoe City were all in the northwest corner of it. They were small ski resorts that people went to on holidays and weekends. South Lake Tahoe had casinos just like Las Vegas. In spite of that, there was a lot of wilderness. The lake did not freeze in winter; it was one of the deepest lakes in the world. It was an ancient glacial lake, very deep and very cold. In May and June you could ski before lunch and in the afternoon go to the beach which was only five miles away. Well, it was even closer in some places. It was perfect! Refreshing year-round, that's for sure.

The family I came to was upper middle class—he was a doctor and she was an artist. They were Swedish-Americans; she was Swedish and he was an American. He had learned Swedish and the children spoke Swedish, so it was a fairly Swedish home and easy to blend in. They had three children, one, three, and five years old, so there was plenty to do all the time. But we had a great time; it was fantastic, really. I don't know what would have happened if I had not felt so much at home there. Maybe I would have lived in Sweden today. A certain amount of chance and good luck entered into it. We are still in touch with each other. Friends for life.

I enjoyed California's climate, the different types of landscape there. You did not have to travel more than a few hours before you came to a completely different environment, and this I found completely incredible. Not just the sun, but that it changes from palms to mountains, from desert to sequoia trees. I saw palm trees in San Francisco and the Golden Gate Bridge, which I had only seen on post cards. It was terrific. So just discovering the state itself was exciting. I traveled a bit, on my own and with the family. Among other places, we went to Hawaii. That held a lot of attraction. I think every Swede dreams about Hawaii! There were so many new things too. I found cars a lot of fun. In Sweden I had not had the time to go skiing, and now I suddenly lived in a ski resort. That was great. I enjoyed that there was so much available, that there was no end to it. If you went shopping, there was so much to choose from. You didn't need everything, but it was still available. Good things and bad things. In a way it added color to life. The supermarkets made a powerful impression on me—the fresh produce section! And the size of the portions in restaurants! And everything was so cheap—gasoline, jeans, records.... The exchange rate was good too; you could buy a dollar for 4.75 *kronor*.

I stayed a year, and after that I suppose I thought that it was time to pack my bag and go back home, even though I didn't really want to. But I had some plans. During my last couple of months in the US I had begun planning a business in Sweden. The concept was a monthly tabloid consisting of nothing but ads. I had been home for three weeks when someone else started *Gula Tidningen* in Stockholm. It was exactly the type of paper I wanted to publish, even though mine would have had a slightly different angle. I had no idea that it was underway, and it was pretty obvious that there was only room for one such publication in Stockholm.

About the same time I realized that I could not start this publication by myself, that I had to find something else. I sat on a bus in Stockholm. Behind the bus driver I saw this announcement: "You haven't forgotten to apply for a rent subsidy, have you?" Or maybe it said "cost-of-living subsidy"—one of the two. It made me so angry. I thought, *What is this?* It's great if there is public assistance available to those who need it, but they shouldn't wave money in front of people's noses. But that is how Sweden was back then. They gave money away to those who wanted it. And I paid taxes for this! I suppose I didn't make that much money then, but I do remember that I paid around 45% in tax that short year I worked in Sweden, and I thought this was completely insane.

Comparing the United States with Sweden was another eye-opener. About this time there was also talk of wage-earners' investment funds, and things looked pretty gloomy to me. I felt that I did not want to be part of this any longer. If I had dreams and ideas, or the simple belief that one should work and be responsible for oneself, then I did not—by paying high taxes—want to provide free money to those who wanted it. Instead, I wanted to see what I could do on my own.

I think weather was a part of it too. Sweden is pretty grey. To live in the snow, if there is snow on the ground, is fine with me. But this grey, dark winter, I found that hard to take. I missed the sun. But most of all: Sweden—and at this time I had seen something of the United States—is small. It is limited. It is good in many ways, but if you are not completely satisfied with it, there is so much more out there in the rest of the world. There are so many more opportunities in the United States; there are no limits. If you want to live in the snow, you can live in the snow. If you want to live in the sun, you can live in the sun. If you work really hard and have some luck, you can do very well economically. The opposite can happen too, of course. But to a greater extent it is up to you. I thought that I would not be as ruled by other people's choices and decisions. And as I said, I did not want to regret something later.

So I made a decision: *OK, I'll save up some money and go back.* I knew that I was welcome back to the family in Lake Tahoe. They said I just had to come back because we had had so much fun. Even on my days off we had spent a lot of time together! It wasn't like a job; we were more like a family. So a year later I went back. I came empty-handed; all I had was two suitcases. This time it felt more definitive, no question about it. You can't be wishy-washy in a situation like this. You can't say that you are going to try for six months or a year, because it may take longer than that. I was going to give it everything I had.

My English was getting better—I had only finished high school and completed my military service—so I did not speak English fluently. English was the subject I liked least. With the start I had, with a whole lot of Swedish spoken around me for the first eighteen-twenty months, it took me a total of three years in the United States to become fully fluent in English. Initially I was exhausted. I managed to express myself, but I stumbled along. There are so many more words in American English. You think you know, then you hear something else, another way of saying something. I often asked:

"How do you say this? Am I supposed to say it this way or that?"

"Well, it doesn't matter." In the beginning, this was pretty confusing. If you don't know the language, it is pretty exhausting, too, when you constantly have to use your head just to get along. It was like going to school every day just to survive, just to move forward. So it took a while, then it started to flow pretty smoothly.

I think Americans believe that if you move here, you should learn English. That's the first thing you do. I also think that most view speaking Spanish or German or Swedish with family and friends fairly sympathetically. As long as you learn English initially, you can communicate and function in society.

Eventually I moved down to San Francisco. There I really had to start from square one! This was perhaps my greatest challenge. I started working in a restaurant, and after a while I thought: *Now that I am working here, I might as well work hard and try to become a manager or something.* Three months later a restaurant in this chain became available and I became the manager of it. I partnered with the man who had hired me and we looked into starting a place of our own. We knew some people with money who were interested, but we never managed to pull it off. So this fellow and I went to Florida instead. Florida was interesting. It was sort of happening then, people were talking about it. For one thing, houses cost only half as much. But it was very difficult initially because there were few well-paying jobs. In the end I ended up working two jobs—one in a restaurant and one in a furniture store.

That's how I got into the furniture business. After a couple of months I quit the restaurant and started working exclusively in the store. It was fun working there, with the exception that the company was about to go under. I saw what was happening and contacted a wholesaler in southern California. So I only stayed in Florida for a year. Since then I have worked for a couple of different companies in the furniture business, among them a Swedish company that sold in Oregon, and through them I learned about the job up here. That was how I met my wife; she worked in one of the stores in Oregon when I came here as a salesman.

I moved to Oregon in early 1990, and then we got married just six months later. That's why I moved here. Before I got married, I had a fair amount of interaction with Swedes. I had met them through work and friends of friends. But when I came here, I did not know any people at all, so as a newcomer to the state I started a new circle of friends—people my wife knew. We have a lot of contact with my wife's family, her parents as well as some other friends. I kept in touch with some people down in California, but I did not feel that I had the same need to see a bunch of Swedes. I don't feel that I have to get together with Swedes just because they are Swedish; at least that's how I felt for a long time. For example, I knew someone in Los Angeles who came from my home town, but we were very different. We had nothing in common except that we both came from Strängnäs, so after a while I totally lost any desire to spend time with him. He was a totally different kind of guy.

I have seen examples of parents who have said that later, when the children reach this or that age, they will start teaching them Swedish. I don't know if some wait because it is too difficult, or because they think it is too confusing for the children. But it does not work. I spoke Swedish to my children from the very beginning. That's the only way. I have continued doing that, but I am a bit lazy at times, since I don't consistently speak Swedish. But I think I can say that I speak Swedish with them every day at least, so they understand it really well. And it has helped my Swedish too, because I had some years when I did not speak very much Swedish and it got a bit rusty. You start throwing in English words ... and you have to stop and think about how to say something correctly in Swedish. I have bought a player that can play Swedish movies, and sometimes we get a CD or a tape from Sweden. I remember that when we first started watching *Pippi Longstocking*, Swedish suddenly became a lot of fun for my kids. My daughter is six years old and I have a son who is two and a half. He says *bil* instead of car, mixes things up a bit, so instead of "car wash" he says "*bil* wash." Things like that are pretty funny.

My wife has Norwegian ancestry and her grandmother is almost more Norwegian than I am Swedish! This grandmother was born in Minnesota, but her parents were from Norway. So she speaks Norwegian. For this reason there are Scandinavian traditions in the family already, like *lutefisk* during Christmas. My wife studied Norwegian in college for a year, and then, since I speak Swedish with the children, she automatically picked it up too. So she understands it fairly well. Maybe not enough to enter into any complicated discussions, but she understands what the conversation is about. When we visited Sweden, she was able to speak some Swedish; she could converse with my father who can't speak English very well. She is very positive about it and it is great to have her support. Otherwise I would feel badly speaking Swedish without her being able to understand anything. In this regard she is behind me 100 percent.

My daughter recently started in the Swedish school,* and that way I meet some Swedes too. It is actually pretty fun. Earlier I didn't feel that much need to socialize with other Swedes, but that has started to change somewhat. I was a bit surprised at how much I enjoyed speaking Swedish again, and we have things in common too. It is possible to discuss things from a different perspective than what I have been used to. We may not spend a whole lot of time together, but it is still fun to see each other. I suppose I can put it this way too: If you are going to do a good job, be a good husband and father and so on, then there isn't much time left over. For this reason, I haven't joined any of the Swedish groups. I haven't felt that my needs have been that great, and I have perhaps become more American than I realize.

You pass through different phases in life. When you are twenty-five or thirty and unmarried, it is fun to live in the sun and play tennis and run around in the evenings. But as you get older, work and family take a really big chunk of time. What's best for the family? It might not be to live in the sun! I have lived in Oregon for almost exactly ten years now. I like it in many ways. Portland is good, and the climate is at least better than Sweden! The summers are much longer and the winters easier. You can drive to the snow if you want, and it is not quite as dark. It is rather Swedish; Oregon's nature is nice. I like the evergreens and I feel more at home here in some way. And people are nor-

---

* The Swedish School in Portland offers classes for Swedish-speaking children on Saturday mornings.

mal and reasonable. I think I have managed to put down roots pretty well here.

If an incredibly good opportunity came along, I would have a very thorough discussion with my wife about it and maybe do something completely different. But I know from when I was a kid myself and had to move—it wasn't always fun. My wife is from here, and that's another part of this equation too. Her parents live two blocks away, her brother lives in Oregon City, her sister in Portland, her grandmother in Lake Oswego. It is very positive to have half the family so close, especially when I have my family over in Sweden. I think it is very important for the children to have these grandparents, aunts and uncles close at hand. I appreciate that, and it is something I would consider very carefully before changing it. If we moved, we would be on our own, and the children would have only us and would have to start over.

I think it is positive that many families here—not all, everyone can't afford it—are able to chose if one parent should stay at home. In our case my wife stays at home with the children, because it is important to us. My mother was a stay-at-home mom; my wife's mother stayed at home, and we value that. We might be able to make more money if she worked, but we think it is important that she stays at home. I don't think that people in Sweden have that choice. I don't know if I can think of a single Swedish family in which both parents don't work. I have to think hard for quite a long time to find a single example. That's too bad. People talk about equality and things like that, but I don't think there is any real fairness when people don't have the opportunity to choose. My personal opinion is that the children need as much time as possible with their parents during their early years. It is a big job, a huge undertaking, and I don't understand how people manage if one of them does not stay at home. My feeling is that it takes all our time, at least for us.

What does my family in Sweden think about my emigration? Well, I think their opinions vary. In general they have said that I probably fit in better in the United States, and that it probably was the right thing for me to do. The most common comment has probably been "Good luck!" My father said: "Well, yes, I would probably have done the same thing." That actually surprised me a little bit. But my mother commented that we became separated even further when the grandchildren were born. Not only that I am gone, but the grandchildren too—an even greater distance between us. Yes, decisions like these are much greater than you think when you are 21 years old. Moving abroad is a fun thing that becomes something much bigger, and you don't think about the consequences that come twenty years later. I have many siblings left in Sweden, and that takes some of the pressure off me. If you are an only child and take off, and your parents grow old, then it is probably difficult.

In general I have to say that it has been positive, but at the same time it has become almost more difficult now, even if I am more established here. I am at home here in so many different ways—yet it is still more difficult somehow because my parents have become older. All my great-grandparents are gone, and there are many gatherings I can't take part in. My children have been there a couple of times, but it is still not a close relationship. There are moments like this when you realize the magnitude of your emigration: *What have I done?* And that your children grow up as Americans—that's another story as well. Are they Americans or Swedes? No, you can't sit there and brood about it; you simply have to make the best of it. During most of my years in the United States I have been in a management position in one way or another for at least ... twelve or thirteen years. This has required that I have sometimes had to make some pretty tough decisions about hiring or firing people, but not even in situations like that has anyone ever said anything about me being Swedish. I have been treated very decently. Unfortunately, it is probably due to the fact that skin color has something to do with it, too—you blend in pretty well here. That is a plus, I suppose. I think Swedes have a really good reputation. I can imagine that the Swedes who came here a hundred years ago worked hard and never became a burden on anyone. A fair number of them came to the Pacific Northwest, so they are not an unknown group. Furthermore, people see the company I work for as Scandinavian, so they are not surprised to see me there either. They basically believe that I arrived with the furniture—more or less on the same ship.

I have to say that people are very positive, and I don't think that anyone has expressed anything negative. They might be curious and a little bewildered as to why I have left Sweden. There are those who are educated and often ask intelligent questions. They can't quite understand why I would leave a country that has such a high standard of living, and that is so beautiful and not very crowded. Then there are those who don't have a clue, of course, and mix up Sweden and Switzerland and many other places, and really don't know anything about Sweden. I would have to say that the majority of Americans know way too little about the rest of the world—including Sweden. The United States is so big that it is "enough" for most Americans. Europe and the rest of the world? Well, Americans don't speak a foreign language and they don't even know what Europe looks like! Many have a very, very narrow view of the world. In addition, Sweden is a pretty small country, and I think Swedes often think it is bigger than it is. They believe that they are more important in the world than they are. But as Swedes, we at least have an awareness of the rest of the world.

Over the years I have lived in many different places, worked different jobs, met a huge number of people in different kinds of situations, encountered many Swedes in the United States, and I have to say that these have been capable, competent Swedes who have left Sweden, for different reasons. In general one would have to say that the Swedes have done well here. If you look at emigration from a Swedish perspective, it is pretty sad really: these are people who could have done a lot of good at home, but who left. And if emigration from Sweden continues every year, it will be a great loss. Maybe it works in the opposite direction as well—that capable foreigners move to Sweden—but something is still weakened somehow. It is unfortunate if taxes, for example, are a major reason behind emigration. I think that Sweden could ease up on a lot of things, be a little bit more open. Not that it matters greatly, or that everyone thinks it is important. Even if I had to start from nothing, hardly knowing the language and not having anything really, and compare myself to my friends back home in Sweden, who went to school, took student loans, and where both parents work—I still have it better financially! But I am no millionaire here, at least not in dollars.

I prefer to take a greater responsibility for my life; I don't want to be pampered. I can decide things for myself. Perhaps this is the biggest problem with Sweden: they say "This is the way to do it!" And almost everyone does it that way. They don't question anything; it is just assumed to be a certain way. Things move along. So much becomes routine that it becomes boring in the long run. Perhaps this is why I feel I fit in better here too: *It is up to me.* It is definitely easier to be an individualist. When I was in high school, it seemed to me that almost everyone looked the same: this is how we dress now; this is popular; this is the music we play. It is pretty much the same for everything all throughout the country. Here, I have never thought that there has been a particular fashion. There are ten different fashions at once, a lot of different musical styles, and large numbers of different groups. There's a tremendous mix, more to sample, more to sink your teeth into.

Sweden feels a lot smaller, and it is easier to just be like the average guy than to go your own way, discover things for yourself, find different possibilities. So I have no problem with the idea that people have to take personal responsibility. I think there is too much pampering in Sweden, that things can get too secure, that people become passive and even lazy. When things no longer suit them, they just start pointing their fingers instead of taking personal responsibility and doing something. I find that attitude hard to accept.

The Swedes who come to America today have made the same choice I did. They could have stayed at home in Sweden—[laughs] now it may sound like I am prejudiced—and just become an average guy. Or, they could have jumped ship to start over somewhere else. And if they move abroad from the security of Sweden, from everything that had already been determined and decided, take the chance to do something on their own—those are individuals with a fair amount of drive, and often an education, who want to get somewhere in the world. So I don't think it is the typical Swede that the Americans encounter: it is individuals who might have that something special, extra, that sense of adventure. I am convinced that this has shaped this country.

I can say that I have become a bit more critical of the United States when it comes to certain things. For example, what's offered on television is often bloody—murders, gunfire, violence and all that—and it upsets me a great deal. If, on the other hand, there are love scenes, nothing is shown and suddenly everything is very hush-hush. In Sweden it is the other way around, and I think that the Swedish view of these things is more natural and healthy. I am also critical of the lack of a geography and foreign language curriculum in the schools. I did not think about this when I first came here; it did not matter to me then. But now that we have children and I look at what they are studying, I have to say that there are things I can point to. But it is difficult to summarize in a few words what the United States is; it is, after all, fifty states. The difference between Oregon and Alabama is enormous! Or even if you compare Oregon to California. For example, recycling has been done for a long time here in Oregon, but has hardly started in other places yet. You discover that this is such an enormous country that it is hard to generalize and be fair at the same time. I don't know if I can find a really good example, but sometimes I am struck by how bureaucratic and complicated things can be here too. This is something people in Sweden complain about, but it is not simple here either. The bureaucracy, filling out forms, is time-consuming, and I don't think I expected this when I first came here.

Unfortunately, you also have to be a little bit more suspicious when you do business in the United States, a little bit more careful. You have to protect yourself, and that is a shame really. In this regard I feel that dealing with a Swede is different. In Sweden it might be sufficient to shake hands and say, "OK, let's do it this way." It might have changed there too, but it still feels more genuine in some way, just to come to an agreement about something. For example, when the Vietnamese come to buy furniture, they'll ask:

"How much is the sofa?"

"Well, it is $1395."

"Can you give me a discount?"

"No, that's how much it is." And then you explain why. Then they ask once more, and then they have to ask yet one more time. It is a completely different way of thinking. This is what they do, and this is what they have always done. They try to bargain on everything. They play this game. If I were one of them, I would do it too, but from the seller's position. Three times I would say that this is the price, but then, the fourth time around, I might lower the price.

In the United States you also have to protect yourself in other ways by getting insurance coverage. I have insurance policies here which I don't think I would even consider back in Sweden. If you were to break your leg and end up unable to work for six months, then there is an insurance policy for that. If a customer were to trip and fall and break his arm, that's the kind of stuff you insure yourself against. Here, a burglar can sue you if he slips on the stairs! Swedes simply shake their heads when they hear these things.

In my profession it is almost like a slogan: *"sell, sell, sell."* There is, of course, a lot more to it than that—people should feel welcome, you don't pressure anyone to buy anything—but that is still what everything revolves around: making money. People here often don't bother to take a vacation, or take too little vacation, or take their job home with them, or work frightfully long hours. I often find people's priorities completely crazy. Now, I have employees—I have been there long enough—so I keep regular office hours more or less, but the store is open seven days a week. That is just the way it is. For you as a consumer, it is good to have it that way, but for the family or society, long hours might not be such a great thing. If the banks are open until three, Monday through Friday, what are people going to do? They have to run around on their lunch break or take a day off to be able to take care of certain things. I don't know how I would manage to do certain things if stores weren't open all the time.

When it comes to vacation—I get three weeks every year as an employee here. Since I am the manager, I can, of course, take an extra day here or there without anyone saying anything. But the overall tempo is higher. I might have slightly better perks than most of the others due to my position, a bit more flexibility, but when you are back home in Sweden talking to people you still notice how much time off they have—weekends, holidays .... That hardly exists here.

To a certain degree I miss the proximity to Europe, to foreign countries. Here you have to travel quite a ways to be able to experience another culture. I miss that more than I thought I would—different culture and history. Our family had a summer cottage in the archipelago outside Stockholm, and we spent our entire summers there. So our summer vacations seemed much longer. We visited there last summer with my children. It was pretty fabulous. I actually miss all the islands and the water; it is not the same here. The same thing is true for Strängnäs—I strolled on the cobblestone streets, went into the cathedral and looked around. You can't find that here, and people don't stroll. It is even somewhat difficult to ride a bicycle in Portland, which is supposed to be such a bike-friendly city.

After twenty years in the United States there are many things I hardly remember about Sweden. If someone asks a question about Sweden, I don't know the answer. I don't know anymore because things have changed so much. Of course, I read Swedish newspapers on the internet more or less every day, even if I sometimes just look at the headlines. At least I won't miss any big news that way. *Aftonbladet* is the newspaper with the most complete coverage, but I also have *Expressen* and *Svenska Dagbladet* bookmarked as well, even *Eskilstuna Kuriren*. In addition, you can go to Yahoo's Swedish site. I normally look at something almost every day. *The Swedish Press* is the only subscription I have here. Occasionally I have asked my family to send me some special magazine, and sometimes I have received Swedish magazines through friends here. I can't say that I keep up with Swedish music—I still have the records I had back in Sweden. Every time I go to Sweden, I buy something, and every now and then I get a CD in the mail, so I probably listen to Swedish music every week.

I don't call Sweden as much now that I use the internet and can send emails so fast. It is mostly to my family. I might call once a month perhaps, to my relatives, birthdays and Christmas and all those things.

Early on I was good at writing letters to old friends back home, and had pretty good response and visitors for many years. But during the last couple of years, everything with the family—many of us had children late in life—takes up a lot of time. So I have lost touch with almost everyone. I have some friends left, but they become fewer and fewer, and our contact, sorry to say, is less and less frequent. Actually I have started feeling, the last couple of years, that I have been gone a while. It was I who disappeared from Sweden; all the others are still there, and their friends are there. Twenty years later it started to sink in that Jan IS gone and won't be coming back. There was a reunion a couple of weeks before I came home. It was the graduating middle school class, twenty-five years later. We could not go because of my daughter's school here. Once before, five or six years ago, there was also some kind of gathering and I went to it. You are quite different from the others attending, because you have lived abroad all these years.

It's fun to come home, nice to see one's family and friends. We went to Sweden last summer, and before that it was five years ago, before that three years, then one year. So it varies. But it gets fairly expensive when you have a family, and I only have three weeks of vacation, and there are also other nice places to go to. We were in Hawaii a year or two before that, and we are going back to Hawaii again this year. Perhaps having the internet makes it a little easier to be away. Furthermore, it is my belief that when you have lived here for many years, you become American even if you don't think so. You lose your footing in Sweden and it does not become quite as important any more. The family is important, but we still keep in touch anyway. I had very, very few visits from my parents and siblings initially, and later the frequency has varied a bit. Many of my siblings have studied and have had different priorities. Traveling becomes a big deal for them too. If they are going to come, it takes a lot of time, because usually they want to see something else too, not just Oregon. It is a long trip that is not exactly cheap.

When I am back home in Sweden, I think it is wonderful to see my family and everything else, and I know that I'm on vacation. The sun is shining and the ice cream tastes good. I might even enjoy some snuff, but then I start thinking: *Would I want to live here? In the fall? Through the winter? And pay these prices every day?* That's when I actually feel like a tourist, like I don't really fit in after all. Towards the end of the trip I begin to feel that I am ready to go home. Truly. And that's here in Oregon.

Sure, one can contemplate moving back to Sweden, discuss it, but when it really comes down to it ... no! I don't think that I could handle it. I think it would be difficult. I have become spoiled in many ways. Even if my wife disappeared out of my life, I would not move back to Sweden. When I retire, I could consider spending the summers there, part of the year. But I don't think that I would like to live there year-round any more. I have it pretty good here.

I am glad that I am not in Sweden now—41 years old, regretting things. If I had felt regret, I could have gone back home. It is that simple. It has not always been easy, and there have been times when things have been much tougher than what I thought they would be. Everything is not perfect. But I did it!

I am a Swedish citizen, and because of that, my children are too. When they turn eighteen, they have three years to decide if they want to continue with their dual citizenship. If I could have dual citizenship, I would take it; I don't see any disadvantages with that. Perhaps there are some advantages with inheritances and things like that, and you get to vote. Definitely. But I think it would be very difficult for me to give up my Swedish citizenship to become an American, because the children are part of the equation too. I might consider it later on, when they have become adults.

I believe that deep down at heart I am Swedish, and will always be Swedish. I can say that I am glad to be Swedish and not American, because I have grown up differently from everybody else here, and there are many things I have learned from that. You just don't throw something like that away. No, I am proud and glad to be Swedish. I don't want to lose that. I will always keep in touch with Sweden; I think it is important. And I want to keep it alive just as much for the children's sake. They are going to learn Swedish, there's no question about it. It is not only this thing about Sweden, but I believe that being bilingual has many other advantages as well. That has been the conclusion of a number of studies. Later on, children learn how to solve problems from different angles because they just don't look at it one way; instead they can think in different channels. And I think it is good for their self-confidence, and that it is easier to learn a third and a fourth language later. But I also want them to understand what it means when I speak with an accent, when I talk about Sweden, when we go to Sweden. It should not be alien to them. And it will, of course, make it possible to keep in touch with their family there. The world shrinks, the European Union and all that—

this is a big deal. I think my children will appreciate being bilingual the older they get.

To be Swedish is perhaps to be more open in your view of other people. I think Swedes are well-informed about the rest of the world, that they are socially ... responsible in some way. I think they are well educated, have a solid foundation. When you look at the shortcomings of the schools here, and with other things, I am glad that I went to school in Sweden. Somehow I want to say that I have learned what is right and wrong—but I don't know if that is Swedish or not .... And this custom that a handshake is often enough, that is probably also pretty Swedish. It is also positive to be different here, that you are not just another American; it is interesting to have a slightly different background, know more about something else, be a little unique! I think people show you more respect too, because as soon as you open your mouth, people understand that you are an immigrant. There is a certain curiosity. Here, I have always seen myself as something of a diplomat too: I want people to think favorably, positively, about Sweden, and I have always tried to live like that.

If I am going to be buried at all, and not have my ashes sprinkled in the Pacific Ocean or something, I really have to consider my family's wishes. I guess they would prefer to have me buried here and not in Sweden, and to me it does not really matter: I am done! It's one of those sentimental things. I remember that my wife asked me about this several years ago, and I had never thought about it before. It caught me off-guard. I was at a loss for words. I can't even recall how I answered. I think I hesitated with an answer for a long time. Finally I said: "I don't know!" I do live here now, and it is a huge step, a definitive step, that I have taken. Strictly speaking, there is no way back. But when it comes down to it, especially now that I have children—children change so much—it has to be here—if I am to be buried at all. I might choose cremation and do what an acquaintance did: have the ashes spread in the sea. I really don't know, but it is not that I have to be buried in Sweden. I must have adjusted pretty well, because this feels like home. Even if I like Sweden in many ways, and there are things there that attract me, and even if I will always be Swedish, I will remain here! I am to a large extent an American too, and have probably put down more roots than I realize.

IV

I Didn't Become Swedish until I Left Sweden

Britt-Mari (b. 1948)

Portland, Oregon, 1998

I met my husband when I was seventeen and a student in a Swedish vocational training school. He was a student at Lewis and Clark College in Portland, Oregon, and he had come to Sweden through a program called "The Experiment in International Living." My husband's group came for five months, staying with a Swedish family and attending a folk high school.* He had not chosen to come to Sweden; the college had selected certain countries. On the other hand he was not uninterested in going to Sweden. A good friend of my mother was the local representative of this organization in southern Sweden, and when

---

* The Scandinavian folk high school movement was founded in 1844 by the Danish minister, author and educator Grundtvig. They function like small junior colleges or vocational schools for young adults (generally from 18 – 25 years old). Most are boarding schools and many are located in rural or small town settings.

he came in April, they had not found a family for him, so he had to stay with this local representative. She felt sorry for him, since her own children were only about ten years old, so she invited me to her house so that he would meet someone his own age. It was good for me to practice my English, and he had the opportunity to learn a little bit of Swedish. That's how we met. It was in 1966.

He traveled around in Sweden and I went up to Stockholm to see him. After that he was supposed to have gone to the Hola Folk High School in northern Sweden, but no one in the group wanted to be up in the "backwoods." Instead, arrangements were made for them to come to Munka-Ljungby in southern Sweden, and immediately it was easier for us to see each other. He returned to America in August. We made no plans to see each other again, and we had not said that we would keep in touch, but there was a feeling that we might. We did not see each other for four years.

He was going to continue his education in the United States. He had been admitted to the University of Washington in Seattle and had started studying law there, but at this time even university students had begun to be called up for Vietnam—initially they had not. Because of this, he had to quit studying and join the military. A year later he came to Germany—it was right before Christmas 1969. I baked ginger snap cookies and sent them to him since he was so far away from home. He was in the middle of some training, so we could not get together. Then I had acute appendicitis in January. He had written that he would call that very same Saturday I had to go to the hospital. My mother was the only one at home. I wrote down what she was supposed to say on a piece of paper. "Can you read this?" I asked. "Yes I can," she said.

But he did not call and it was a great disappointment. But he did call later, and for Easter 1970, when I was well again, he came to Sweden. We had not seen each other since August 1966. He was supposed to stay in Germany for two years. It was very convenient to live in Malmö then, because I could pack my suitcase on Friday, put it in a locker at school, and then go to Copenhagen directly after school to catch the night train that arrived in Germany Saturday morning. Then I returned from Germany Sunday afternoon and arrived just in time for school Monday morning. We also met in Holland at the house of his mother's parents. Whenever he could, he came to Sweden. He had bought a Volvo, his first car. We got engaged in September 1970 and were married on Midsummer Day in 1971. The marriage was held in Nässjö, the town of my birth. His parents, his maternal grandparents, a couple of his parents' friends from Portland, and some friends from the military in Germany had come. Then there were my parents, relatives, and the Swedish friends we had in common. After our wedding, I stayed in Sweden and completed my last term at the teachers' training college, and in December 1971 he also finished his military service.

We had no long-term plans. It was advantageous to get married while he was in the military because, when he was done, he could choose a so called "European Out." That meant that he could stay in Europe for another year, and the US military would still pay for his moving expenses back to the United States and, as a result of having married, that payment included me and our belongings. We lived together for a year in Malmö in the notorious Rosengård suburb where all the immigrants and Swedish welfare recipients lived. My husband worked in a language school teaching English, and I worked there too, teaching Swedish. In Malmö I also worked as a substitute teacher in upper elementary schools and have a feeling that I must have visited every single school at some point. It was quite enjoyable and instructive. Among other things, I got to experience different approaches and the different atmospheres of the schools. I suppose we considered settling in Sweden, but my husband did not seriously look into studying law in Sweden, because he would have had to supplement a great deal.

My husband wanted to continue with his law studies in Seattle, and in August 1972 we moved to the United States. At that point he had been admitted to the University of Washington. We would live there for at least three years. We thought that once he was done, we might return to Sweden. I had never been to the United States. My parents and siblings never said that they didn't want me to move, even though I know that they would have liked me to be closer. One of my brothers cried when I left that first time—we who could argue and get mad at each other. He thought it was difficult. My other brother did not say anything, but I heard later that he thought it was more or less like me being dead when I was so far away. It was very difficult for my mother and for my father, but they did not say very much to me. They were encouraging and thought that it would be interesting for me to go abroad. In those days you never called! Only in a matter of life or death would you make a phone call and convey the most important things. I had not understood how far Seattle was until I left.

I actually wanted to go to college in the United States,

but it was very expensive. It wasn't a common thing to do in those days precisely because the costs were so prohibitive. My parents thought that they, as a kind of compensation, would host American youths in our home. The same year my husband was in Sweden, we had a girl from Mississippi staying with us through the summer. In 1969 we had another girl from California. These visits turned out to be very successful; we still keep in touch and call each other "sister." We are very close even though we don't see each other that often. They adjusted well to our family and they had a good time in Sweden. So as a result of this, I had been in close contact with Americans and had become better at speaking English and learning about the United States.

I knew many young Americans because I had traveled with youth groups associated with the local representative for "The Experiment in International Living." In addition, I had worked for the American man who ran the language school; he was from Louisiana and had emigrated in the other direction. He was black and had no desire to return home. He gave a more negative view of the United States. On the other hand, he did not like Sweden that much either; his opinion of Sweden was rather negative as well. Through my American "sisters" I think I got the impression that the United States was more or less like Sweden since we seemed to have so much in common. To a certain degree this is true: if you look at daily life, the differences there are not very big. But any more than that—I had not given much thought to how it would be. I had never flown in an airplane before. Because the military was in charge of our move, we were able to take everything with us, including old furniture which I hardly thought worth keeping. In the US they suddenly became valuable. Twenty-five years ago there was so much plastic and polyester. I was not prepared for so much junk. It surprised me greatly.

In Seattle we started looking for an apartment. In Sweden I had moved from a rural area to a city neighborhood of single-family houses. To have to live in an apartment in Rosengård was bad enough. But those apartments were new; they had a refrigerator and a freezer and the standard was high. They were simply luxurious compared to what I saw in Seattle. Those in Seattle had thick wall-to-wall carpets and the smell was awful. The places were not particularly clean. But my husband, who had lived in apartments when he was a student, had experienced places that were even worse. He thought that the apartments he showed me were pretty nice.

My husband's aunt and uncle lived in Seattle. It turned out that we had a lot in common. They suggested that I should sign up with the Scandinavian Department at the University of Washington, which I did, and that is how I got in touch with them. I taught at the Swedish Club, in their Evening Class curriculum, and in a multi-cultural program in the schools. The membership of the Swedish Club consisted of mostly older people—some Swedes who had emigrated a long time ago, but primarily second generation Swedish-Americans. Through one of my husband's fellow students, we got to know Ulf Beijbom and his family from the House of Emigrants in Växjö. He was a visiting professor at the University of Washington at this time. They lived close by, and it turned out that their children, having recently arrived in the United States, needed some help with their English. I suppose it was through him that we came to attend the events of the Swedish Club and many of those Scandinavian or Swedish organizations up in that area. Before I came here, I didn't know that something like this existed, or that I would have a use for my Swedish teacher training in the United States. We were active in student life and made friends from around the world. It was a slightly different atmosphere than if we had come directly to Portland. Our friends, just like us, were there studying for the time being, and the atmosphere among students is different. The years in Seattle turned out to be a lot of fun, and we are still in touch with many of our friends from that time.

When my husband had completed his studies, he received a Fulbright scholarship and we moved to Stockholm. That's where our second son was born. We lived for a year in a student apartment in an area called Bergshamra. The apartment was nothing but a big chunk of concrete, but I thought the area was nice. Stockholm has incredibly beautiful surroundings. In the Ulriksdal forest you can pick mushrooms and go skiing. You can ice skate on Edsviken. I worked as a language teacher for immigrants and traveled the city on the subway. My husband attended Stockholm University, the faculty of law, where he studied international law. I thought that Stockholm was really nice, which I did not when I lived nearby as a child. I actually felt at home there. Before leaving Seattle we had decided that we were not going to stay. And we did not change our plans, so when he finished in June 1976, he had to find a job. We started to feel that we really had to make a decision about where we were going to settle down. We had two children and we were almost thirty years old. We had talked about the possibility of settling in Holland, and my husband had gone there, but nothing came of it. His parents were pushing for us to return to the United States, and they thought that there were greater opportunities here, which, in his case, definitely was true. We decided that he would go to the United States first to look for a job, and when he found one, we would follow. I would stay in Malmö over the summer with the children, and come in the fall. But my stay turned out to be a full year, because he had still not found a job that fall, and he did not get one until the next spring. He lived with his parents in Portland and looked for work in different parts of the United States. Finally he landed a job with Pacific Power in Portland, and accepted it. That was in the summer of 1977. I came in September with the boys. He had visited Sweden over Christmas, and we had tried to follow up on some contacts we had for a possible job in Sweden. I suppose you get a bit more worried when you have children to take care of, you don't have much patience for waiting, and you feel that it is better not to take any chances.

The move to Portland turned out to be my greatest culture shock. That is when I arrived completely to the United States, to Americans. Sure, I had lived in an apartment before, but our circle of friends had been students. It had been international. For me, these contacts had been very stimulating. I felt completely isolated in Portland, and I thought that my first year was horrible. I was incredibly depressed. I did not want to live in Portland. In those days Portland's river front was very ugly. I did not think that there was any culture to speak of either. Malmö was not that big, but Malmö had a concert hall, a symphony orchestra, and many visiting performers. I thought that it was incredibly boring here. The first time I had seen Portland was when we came to the United States in 1972. We stayed for six weeks before moving on to Seattle. In addition, I had visited my parents-in-law on a few weekends. Our three years in Seattle was more like an interlude in our lives. I probably have to say that 1977 was the year of my definitive emigration, and it was much more difficult. I knew that we ought to stay put, and that it was the most practical thing to do since my husband could get the best jobs here. Even if I liked my job as a teacher, I did not want to be the one supporting the family. We could always move from Portland after a couple of years—once my husband had gained some experience and better positioned himself for a new job somewhere else.

Our oldest son was five years old when we came to Portland, and he always asked: "Mom, where are the children?" He was used to the playgrounds in Sweden, which were full of kids, and where all he had to do to find friends was to go there. But here he made no friends, because the children only waved to him through the window. They were never outside. But then we met a small girl whose mother came from Mexico, and she became my best woman friend. We had a lot in common and our children were the same age. So then he had a friend who also liked to play outside.

The mothers I met later on were not the type of women I had known earlier. As a Swedish woman I always felt that I had more in common with men than with women. The American women with beautiful hair and make-up were often much more "elegant" than I was. At that time, this was much more conspicuous. They were like Barbie dolls, and I had never been that. Then they spent so much time talking about their husbands, and I could not understand that. Many of the women I met did not have any interests other than their husband and children. They did not work—and there's nothing wrong with that at all; I did not work either—but you can still have other interests. I was not really able to converse with them. They were on their way home to watch the soap operas and so on, and I detest that kind of thing. For me, this was the great collision with the United States; I felt like an outsider and very different.

In this neighborhood I also discovered a class distinction which I had not noticed before. People who lived in this area had slightly more money than those who lived in the apartments a bit further away, and if you walked past the other side of the school, the houses were much, much larger and nicer and those who lived there had still more money. We felt that we had things which did not belong to the class of our neighborhood. We drove a Saab and in this area no one owned a European car. I also dressed like someone who had more money than what we had, but I dressed like a Swede. And in those days there was a greater difference between the clothes you could buy here and in Sweden. Today there is no difference. It was a bit strange, because I felt that my clothes colored people's perception of me. Judging my external appearance they thought that I belonged to a certain class. Economically, I certainly didn't; I was in the same situation as they were. I still think that people live and work in a very segregated way, and that new suburban areas consist of people of the same age who are on the same economic level.

During the first five years I thought mostly about how to endure until we could figure out what to do next. On the other hand, I really wasn't the kind of person who wanted to move right away either. Then the oldest boy started school. I liked the school; I liked his teacher, and naturally I had something in common with her since I was a teacher myself. Somehow Swedish descendants learned that I was a Swedish language teacher and they contacted me and wanted to study Swedish. So I started giving Swedish classes in my home and things immediately started looking up. That way, I met people, both men and women, who shared my interests.

That I began to feel at home here was probably also related to us buying a house and actually settling down, putting down roots. As a result of having moved around a fair amount as a child, I have probably always been slightly rootless—one who waits for the next move. So to safeguard yourself, because it is difficult to leave, you don't become so involved. Things are easier if you think of yourself as a stranger who is only there for a short time and who doesn't get too involved in anything, and doesn't get attached. So the adjustment had something to do with my own attitude, too. In those days my mother and father were often here and sometimes stayed for six weeks, sometimes as long as three months. That was a lot of fun. My father worked on the house and in the garden, and my mother helped in the house. That increased the feeling of being at home. I noticed that they sometimes felt more at home here than I did; that was a bit strange. But then I realized that I had to try a little myself too, and make sure that I would feel at home, not just constantly think about moving away from here. At that time, Portland began to change and become a little bit nicer, which also influenced my feeling of well-being.

My contacts with Swedes were, I suppose, somewhat random. The Swedes I met when I first came here had left Sweden for different reasons than me. I met some, for example, who said that they "had escaped from communism in Sweden." Many of these Swedes also seemed to think that everything Swedish was bad and everything American was good. One can certainly wonder why they had to think that: *Maybe it was impossible for them to return? Maybe they came from unfortunate circumstances?* What they had experienced and spoke about I could agree with, but you don't have to dislike something old just because you like something new. I am more ambivalent myself and think that there are good and bad things in both places. Initially I only saw the bad aspects of the United States and the things I liked in Sweden. I had forgotten that there were many things I did not like when I lived there. Over the years I have developed a more nuanced view which I find that I am continuously re-evaluating.

There was a lady, a Norwegian, who had a Scandinavian shop when I first came to Portland, and she was very sweet and kind. She kept a list of names of Swedes, Norwegians, Danes, and so on, and when you came into her shop she would say: "Perhaps you would like to meet so and so?" She was a great contact. For Christmas we had our Swedish Christmas lights and Advent Star in the window, and then there was a Norwegian woman who had walked past and realized that I was Swedish or Scandinavian. She also noticed me when I walked the neighborhood with my baby carriage, which no one else ever did here. People knew who I was; I could meet people in the store who said: "Oh, it's you! I have seen you walk by with your baby carriage." So that is how I met the Norwegian woman, and it sort of happened by itself. We attended a few Swedish events, but I don't recall that we spent a great deal of energy on them. I knew this from my years in Seattle—these organizations consist mostly of

Swedish-Americans, and they don't have the same background I do.

I often feel that I have more in common with the young Swedes I meet. They seem to absorb what is good and ignore what is bad in a different way, and not just say, "Well, if this is American it has to be good. And that, that's Swedish and we have left that behind. It's no good." They go back home much more frequently and they want their children to be bilingual. In my generation there are not that many families in which the children speak Swedish. I also think that the younger Swedes are more open, because if they find something that is better than what they have here, well, then they will move to Sweden, or move somewhere else. They have preserved what is positive about Sweden.

My Dutch mother-in-law thought that we should keep our traditions. She always said: "Bring your own traditions with you, because there are none here!" And the funny thing is that, this far away from Sweden, the Swedish traditions appear relatively similar to the Dutch ones. The food is the same, and they hand out presents on Christmas Eve. That suited my husband, because that's what they had always done. I was definitely bound by tradition earlier, much more than anyone else in my family, and this was intensified when I came to the United States. It was something from home that gave a sense of security. I suppose you can say that I didn't become Swedish until I left Sweden.

I have a new Swedish cookbook, but Swedish food today is so international. When we were children, we ate basic, traditional Swedish food, but when we moved south to Skåne my mother simplified her cooking a great deal.

She stopped baking and stopped canning. My mother is much more modern than me in that regard. Early on, I baked everything, cooked everything, did everything myself. I make pea soup sometimes because my family likes Swedish food. I always buy full grain rye bread in a German store. We never eat "foam rubber bread" and at home I always keep *knäckebröd*,[†] Swedish cheeses, caviar, and pickled herring. I like fish, but I don't cook herring or old recipes like that; I like more modern recipes that I find in Swedish magazines. Sometimes I make thin Swedish pancakes, both the large and the small kind. We buy big containers of lingonberries in Ballard in Seattle. Sometimes we go up there to stock up certain things. We also love Swedish candy. We stockpile that when we go to IKEA or when we go to Sweden. I always bake for Christmas, and a small cake occasionally ... It feels a bit barren if you don't have anything at home. In Sweden you are always used to serving something with the coffee. Serving a cup of coffee without anything to go along with it—you simply can't do that! There has to be something—a bun, a slice of cardamom bread, something.

Something I have become aware of in the United States, and which frightens me, is that people here—in my opinion—don't have a social conscience. People don't feel any responsibility for others. You put out your bags of discards, and organizations come and pick them up, or you write a check that you can deduct from your taxes. But that *you* should have to pay for *other* people's children to attend good schools, or that other people's children should receive daycare from qualified personnel when their par-

---

† Traditional Swedish rye crisp bread.

ents are at work—well, Americans think people have to pay for that themselves. "I shouldn't have to pay now that my kids are grown! I have done my share!" Comments like these worry me greatly. And similarly, that you pay to help the elderly. I believe that we have a common responsibility. And this is not just me. Sometimes this surfaces when I speak with other Scandinavians too. I am fully convinced that this is a Scandinavian mindset. But if you say that, you are to this day perceived as a communist or at least a socialist. But I don't feel like a socialist at all. In Sweden I was conservative; here I am incredibly liberal.

When our children were small and played nude in a pool, the neighbors got very upset. The landlord received anonymous phone calls. It was just ridiculous. Another thing that surprised me when I came here was the double moral standard. Here everything appears so nice—father, mother, and children, and you go to church on Sunday and everything looks perfect. But things are not any different than they are in Sweden. My experience is that people in Sweden are more honest about the things that deviate from the moral norm. We admit that they exist. Americans, for example, can't understand this thing about living together without being married. I don't have any statistics about cohabitation, but my guess is that it is as common here, but it is not generally accepted. Students often ask about this.

What Americans know about Sweden depends on their level of education. If I think about the parents I met in the schools when my children grew up, they generally knew nothing, not even where it is. Today, Americans, just like the Swedes, travel much more. For that reason it is more common that people have been to Scandinavia.

Young parents today are perhaps better informed about other countries. You often meet someone who has hosted an exchange student from Sweden. Americans are interested in the social aspects of Sweden—the entitlement programs, health care, and care of the elderly. At the same time they wonder how one can possibly pay so much in taxes. You almost always get that question. It irritates me that when Americans talk about Sweden, it sounds so cute and charming, but that one could not possibly live in a country like that. It is only a picturesque place that you go to visit. It is somehow not real ....

I can't say that I have experienced any downright prejudices. It has happened that people have thought that Sweden was a communist country. I had neighbors who believed that you were not allowed to move and live where you wanted. A lot of people also show curiousity and interest. A couple of women who were colleagues of my husband were interested in hearing about Swedish day care and things like that. All of this made me feel very different. The first time I came to the United States, I actually made an effort to become more American, even though it is not really possible to remake yourself. You are the person you are.

When I first came to the United States, I thought that I would find great freedom and individualism, but the longer I live here, the more I find that assumption completely wrong. Look at the children for example: they all pass through grade school, middle school, high school. And then, if you are academically interested, you go to college. This is true for this entire, enormous country! Following the same pattern is not particularly individualistic. My own schooling was certainly varied. Then there are many more regulations here than you would guess, for all kinds of things, such as building permits. There are regulations in our neighborhood and we are not, for example, allowed to have a fence in front of the house. I feel like a Swede living abroad, not like an emigrant. I did not choose to leave Sweden in order to live in the United States; circumstances brought me here. I could consider living almost anywhere. That's what makes me feel like a Swede living abroad, and I will probably always feel that way. But much has changed. Perhaps the fact that people know a little bit more about Sweden makes it feel more positive. You don't always have to explain, because that gets tedious in the long run; even positive interest gets tedious in the end. You get used to it, of course. You don't see all the differences any more either. This is a huge country. There are many opportunities. If you think about the children, they can end up anywhere.

Earlier, people in Sweden always looked up to authority figures—it was the teacher, the doctor and so on. Here, perhaps, people don't look up to people in authority positions ... I mean, I am not impressed by people's titles or the amount of money they have. You speak with another person because they are another human being, and you respect them for what they are. You don't remain silent because you don't dare address someone because he or she is a person of authority. Perhaps I dare to be more outspoken, or be more open, after having lived in the United States. It is hard to say, because so much has changed in Sweden too.

My husband speaks Swedish. It is actually related to his mother wanting him to learn Dutch. She came here right after World War II, but at that time being bilingual was not as accepted as it is today. It was not considered necessary. My father-in-law asked: "Why should we speak Dutch?" And, of course, he did not speak it himself. She had bought books, but not until the children were ready for school. At that point they were not interested. So she spoke from personal experience and said that it was better to start from the very beginning. But when she got sick and my husband's uncle came here from Holland, his English was not that good. He became very frustrated when he did not understand everything that happened to her when she was sick and dying, and we could not explain. She was so sick that she did not always have the strength to speak to him and explain everything. And she was the only one who knew Dutch. Things like this have played a part. It would have been good if we had been able to speak with him in his own language.

My parents don't speak much English. Very early on I thought that if I had children one day, and it was a bilingual relationship, I would like them to speak the language of both their parents. When our children were young, I made a point of always speaking Swedish to them, and we still often do that. But since the children are so old now—two are grownups—discussions will develop about things where they lack a Swedish vocabulary, and I can't give them that. They can only get that through personal experience. In those situations we switch over to English. You can't become tongue-tied just because you don't have those words. My husband's Swedish has always been good, but because he visits Sweden so rarely, it has become more difficult for him to express himself, even if he understands a great deal. English becomes easier.

Our children are Swedish citizens; they have Swedish

passports and can work in all the European Union countries. They have great opportunities, which is very interesting. It might not be necessary for them to live in Sweden, but I do think that they feel partly Swedish after all. One son was born in Stockholm, but he is the one who has spent the least amount of time in Sweden. When people ask him, he always says that he is Swedish, that he was born in Stockholm. Our youngest son, oddly enough, spoke English with a Swedish accent when he was little, but that has disappeared now. He enjoys being in Sweden a great deal. In Sweden he can have much greater freedom as a child than anyone can give him here. Things have changed here, unfortunately. Earlier the children always rode their bicycles to their friends; now they are almost always driven, so of course that gives them a feeling of being restrained and limited. People are scared ... there have been incidents of children being molested. This is a society where people move around a lot, so you can't be secure even if you live in a good neighborhood. I have never researched this scientifically, but I have always maintained that IF mothers spent more time outside with their children, IF more people were outside, things would be less dangerous. In Canada, if you go to Vancouver, you can walk outside at all hours. People are outside around the clock. When we go there, our children say, "Oh, it is almost like Sweden."

I am close to my Swedish family and relatives. We don't call each other that often, we don't write that often, but when we see each other, we have so much in common. It is as if we have never been apart. How frequently I have traveled back to Sweden has varied. Lately it has been more often, because my parents have become so old that they have stopped traveling. Something could happen at any moment. You start thinking: *No, we won't wait until next summer, because you never know. We better go now.* In the 90s, I went to Sweden every other year or so, but earlier it could be as long as four years. Once I did not see my oldest brother for six years. He lived up in the north of Sweden and we came to Skåne in the south, and we didn't have a chance to see each other. But my experience with him was the same: When we met it was like, "Well, hi there!" It seemed more or less like yesterday. We have not had very many visitors. My brothers have never been here, for example. I have an aunt who has been here twice and cousins who have been once each. We don't even have visitors once a year; it is very irregular. Naturally, it would be fun if we could see each other more frequently, but on the other hand I don't feel homesick and constantly long for them. I did initially, but that was mostly because I was afraid that we would not be able to keep in touch. Now I know that we will stay in touch and that this connection will not suddenly disappear. Knowing that, you can live with distances.

Family life in Sweden is something natural; here it is not always taken for granted. One difference is that the generations sit together at the dining table in Sweden. Here, among the Americans we know, the children sit by themselves, and when they get to be teenagers, they are no longer included in social invitations. Then you have to ask if it is OK for them to come along. And there is often something planned for the children so they have something to do, and I don't know that we do that in Sweden. At least we never did. The children play in a natural way or sit with the adults. Furthermore, we have never had the "Rules of Our House" defined, or a division of labor. When I came to the United States, I took a couple of parenting classes to see how they were, and then it was always considered very important to have this division of labor in the home so that the children had their share. I don't know if American families generally do this, or if it is just something that is taught in classes. In Swedish families, each and every one commonly does what is needed when it is necessary. You simply help each other.

When I came here, I was asked if I wanted to teach Swedish at Portland State University—without pay. For a couple of years I said "No thank you," but then I finally began teaching there in 1983—with a salary. If you compare working here with working in Sweden, the biggest difference is—because I work part-time—that you don't receive any health care or retirement benefits. There are no full-time positions in our field. In addition, our contracts run from one term to the next, so we are always like newly hired employees. There is no job security. Your years of service don't add up to anything, and the unions have very little to say. In my case, when it comes to the work itself, it is very independent. I teach my classes in the evenings and I don't participate much in the life of the university in the daytime. My classes always have mixed ages, but maybe there are slightly more, younger students now. I had 24 students in the largest class I ever taught. Working in the foreign language department suits me perfectly, because I meet a very international group of people there. The Scandinavian teachers stay especially close. We meet regularly once a month and we have stuck together when it comes to our terms of employment, contracts, and things like that. Our common Scandinavian view becomes apparent there.

I have basically been a housewife who has worked in

the evenings, and I have been fortunate to work with what I was trained for. Now we also have the Swedish School, and I find that enjoyable because the younger Swedes involved there have a view of Sweden and the United States that is similar to mine. The younger ones are much more international and open than our generation. They are easy to talk to. For me, the Swedish School reconnects me with my first job as a grade school teacher, and I think it is fun to be able to activate that again.

The Swedish-American organizations uphold the culture that came with the emigrants long before me. They convey the heritage of my grandparents' generation, a heritage I don't share. I sort of see them as the grandchildren of Karl Oskar and Kristina, the main characters in Vilhelm Moberg's emigration novels, and I think of the Swedish-American poet Arthur Landfors, and so on. And Swedish-American Swedish is different as well; there are dictionaries for it and they use words we no longer use in modern Swedish. In a way I find it interesting to see what has survived, but it's not today's Sweden. It is not my Sweden.

I don't belong to any Swedish organization, unless you count the Swedish-speaking women's group that gets together for coffee. It is a loosely affiliated group. We don't really have a membership fee. We pay ten dollars for postage, because every month we send out an invitation about where we are going to meet. We gather for the sole purpose of speaking Swedish. Anyone is welcome, but they have to understand that we speak Swedish so they don't feel excluded. It is important to have the opportunity to speak Swedish, and the language itself is an aspect of my professional interest too. It feels essential to maintain it.

And we exchange a few magazines and books. We meet at someone's home. Our membership roster has 70 – 80 names, even though we are not that many when we meet. We might be ten or twenty people who get together. The vast majority are Swedish. There are a few exceptions, but everybody speaks Swedish. We give each other suggestions about places that sell Swedish things and so on.

I subscribe to *Femina*, which is a magazine for women that, among other things, reviews new books and has articles about authors, which I enjoy reading. The Swedish Institute provides me with the magazine *VI* during the academic year, and I read that. My husband sometimes buys the newspaper *Dagens Nyheter* in Portland. It is interesting to read about the United States from a Swedish point of view, for example. I read Swedish every day. I am a member of the organization *Riksföreningen Sverigekontakt*, and I have belonged to Bonnier's Book of the Month Club since sometime in the 70s.

I have always said that I will move back to Sweden when I get old. When I was twenty, I was on a study tour in Österlen in southern Sweden, and I said: *This is where I want to live when I get old!* But the other day I thought: *But the winters are so cold! Perhaps it would be nice to live there during the summers.* But considering pensions and everything else, I don't know if I would be able to, and it also depends on if my husband would want to live there, or if it would be just me. It has always been in my mind that if I ended up alone for some reason, I would move back to Sweden with the children. Government support policies for families make life so much easier for single parents in Sweden. As a teacher I would get a better job in Sweden since I don't have an American teacher's education. But that is no longer guaranteed, because I have an old teacher's certificate and I haven't worked in Sweden for many years. I have begun to wonder if returning might be unrealistic. I am not an American citizen and I have not considered becoming one. I have not thought it necessary. Sometimes it irritates me that I can't vote; that's the only thing. It would be strange to travel on a US passport, but that is probably only an emotional consideration. In addition, I have found it a good thing to have one foot in Sweden and one here by being married to an American—greater possibilities if we would like to move between the two.

I have always said that I don't care what happens to me when I am dead. I am alive now, and when I leave my life on earth, those who remain can do what they want. We visited Malmö last summer and my son, father, and I went to a concert in the church in Husie, the church of our old congregation. It was a beautiful summer evening. The Husie church—a whitewashed church on top of a hill—has a Danish stair-turret, and towards evening the sun shines so beautifully on it that all the surfaces sparkle. Then I thought, when we walked up to it, that the memorial grove there would be a good place for my ashes. I haven't decided anything, but I have thought about it. I think it would feel good to know that my ashes would rest there, but I really don't care what happens after that.

V

I FELT EXACTLY AS IF I HAD
STEPPED INTO A MOVIE

Herje (b. 1954)

Hillsboro, Oregon, 1998

The first time I came to the United States was shortly
after landing my first job. I had been a student at Chalmers, the technical university in Gothenburg, and they had a
"USA group" that assisted students with trainee positions
in the States. I'm sure it would have been fun to be part
of that, but I wasn't enough of a go-getter to get involved.
I was fully occupied with everything else—parties, music, a bit of studying now and then .... Anyway, I got my
degree and started working as a computer engineer for a
consulting firm in Gothenburg—hardware, software, development. When I had worked there for about a year, we
became the distributors for Oregon Software, their Pascal
compiler. This was in the era before PCs. We imported
this from Oregon to Sweden and Norway, and I became
the contact person and worked with marketing and adver-

tising. I made a lot of phone calls. We used the compiler ourselves, but whenever I could not answer a question, I had to call or send a fax to Oregon to get an answer. So I developed contacts, and my first trip to the United States was actually to Portland to attend an international distributors' meeting that Oregon Software arranged. That was in 1982. I attended at least two such meetings before I moved here. The visits lasted a few days or a week. Very enjoyable. They took such great care of me, better than they ever would have in Sweden, and they showed me around privately so I got to see things.

On my first trip I also took a week's vacation and went down to Los Angeles to visit a guy I knew from my days as a student at Chalmers. He worked down there. I went to Universal Studios and ended up behind two girls who spoke Swedish. We started talking and got to know each other a little bit, and exchanged addresses and phone numbers. They were going to hitchhike up to San Francisco and continue to Hawaii. Eventually, a few months later that summer, I picked up a copy of *Expressen*, the evening newspaper, and saw two photographs on the front page: I had seen these faces before! They were those two girls! They had gone missing and were later found murdered. Hitchhiking, they had been dragged out into the woods and murdered. This affected me a bit, because it was the first time I had actually known somebody who ended up a murder victim, even if I did not know them that well.

I suppose that this incident did not influence my view of the United States in a way that stayed with me, but it was an image I guess—I don't know if I already had it back then—but I do now: The United States is a pretty violent country. There are many crazy devils here, but they can be found in other countries too. There are a lot of guns and some very extreme people. I think there are more extreme people here than in many other places. This is a violent society in general, but Sweden is pretty violent too when you think about it, especially in the big cities. But the violence in America was not anything that frightened me off, even though I thought it was incredibly stupid for two girls like that to hitchhike.

I remember the first time I landed in the United States—guards, customs officials with pistols, and there was probably a sheriff somewhere too, and I thought: *Wow, the Wild West!* And then, when we drove through east Portland on our way downtown where Oregon Software was located, I thought that it looked so trashy somehow. I felt exactly as if I had stepped into a movie, because I had seen those kinds of environments in so many television series and films. And as I looked out through the car window to take it all in, it was suddenly just like that—all the little details, signs, gas stations and restaurants. Then there were quite a few old junker cars parked; it wasn't as neat and tidy as it is in Sweden. And there were traffic signs and phone lines along the streets that you don't find in Europe. The sum of all those things made me feel as if I was traveling around inside a film. That's exactly how it was.

Customs officials have always been somewhat difficult. They are tough. Now, after getting my residency visa, it has been fine; but earlier, during one of these visits, they took me aside and made me talk about electronics. My English was not that good either. I did alright, I spoke tourist English, but when I started talking about *business visit* and *electronics,* they took me into one of these rooms on the side and made me empty my pockets. They thought

I was going to smuggle electronics. What was so stupid was that I was on my way *into* the United States; what they were concerned about was electronics being taken *out of* here. I never understood that. It turned out alright in the end; nothing came of it. But it was upsetting because I was young and green and wondered what I had gotten myself into.

I liked the food and the bars—all that was very nice. Those were positive impressions, definitely. I rented a car and expected the traffic to be difficult. I was a little bit nervous about driving in the US; I guess I thought it would be tough. I had seen movies from New York with people screaming and car chasing scenes and things like that. And then traffic was the slowest I had ever experienced! And friendly! People let you in and it did not go very fast, and the car was an automatic and driving it was easy and comfortable. Driving was easier than in Gothenburg! And I like to read maps so I eventually found my way around. Not at once, of course, but after a while.

In 1984 my boss called me and asked what I had going on, if I wanted to go to the United States on a project. It was a week's notice, maybe two, and the project was estimated to last for at least three months. There was some talk that there might be something after that, but three months was for sure. It did not take long to get a visa at the consulate; it was stamped into my passport at the last minute, on my way out to the airport. I got an L-1 visa, work for a subsidiary, which is a bit special. It was an easy visa to get, but it was limited to that one company. You couldn't take another job. At that time, when I came to Portland, there were already three Swedes here who eventually went back. They did not live here when I came to that first distributor's meeting; they had come later and started the company. It was just a room with a shared secretary. The company also had a furnished apartment, and the idea was that people would come, stay, do a project, then go back. All of this was in Beaverton. One fellow lived there with his wife when I arrived, so I was put in another apartment in the same complex with some borrowed furniture, boxes and things like that. After a couple of months they returned home and I moved into that apartment.

Some financial turbulence developed in the Swedish company after a while, and they wanted me to come back home again. But I wanted to stay and continue that year. We argued a little bit about that. Eventually the company was bought by a bigger computer company in Sweden, and they were going to invest in us over here. We would continue as a subsidiary to them. They came to Oregon and everything was so positive. But as it turned out, they did not spend anything on us—no investments and no expansion. So we started getting a bit irritated about this. We worked hard; we were ambitious. A fair amount of money went back to Sweden. I wasn't that involved in the inner workings of it all, but in the end we bought our company back and paid off some investment debts. That's how we became an independent company here, owned by us. But that did not last either, and eventually we too split up. We continued working on the contracts we had and I stayed on as an independent contractor for Cascade. After a couple of years I had been an independent contractor for Cascade for so long that they could not keep me on any longer— either I had to become an employee or do something else. So I became an employee, and I am still there today.

Initially I did not do anything about my condo in Sweden, but later I rented it to the sister of a friend. She studied at Chalmers for a year, then, as it became obvious that I would not move back for a while, I sold it. It was certainly a big step. Maybe I should have held on to it longer, because its value was going up. Still, I did not lose any money when I sold it either. And I thought that if I was going to move back to Sweden, I would like something bigger. It was just a studio and nothing special.

When I sold my place in Gothenburg, I did not have very much furniture. With the help of friends and parents some of it was sold, and I had a couple of boxes of stuff sent over to Oregon. I had moved into a furnished apartment, so I had what I needed. I had some boxes of books sent over and my parents stored the rest. During my visits to Sweden over the years, I have brought more and more of my small childhood things, so they eventually end up here. On my last trip from Sweden I brought so many heavy things that one suitcase got too heavy—I had to re-pack right there at the check-in. A heavy microscope from my childhood came along that time.

Then I bought a condo in Beaverton—two bedrooms, a hallway, a kitchen and a back yard. About 1000 square feet. When I had bought it, I felt that I was somewhat stuck here, that I would have to sell something before I could move again; I couldn't just stop renting. That was probably a bigger step than getting rid of the condo in Sweden. It was the first root: buying a piece of property. You acquire possessions and one thing is added to the next. You are no longer as flexible.

Another side of this story is that when I was given this opportunity to go the United States, I was really sick and tired of Gothenburg. I thought that everything had sort of stagnated. I was a bachelor. There was nothing exciting happening. A lot of my life was a go-to-work routine. It was not very enjoyable. It was time for a change, so it was great fun to come here. The first two or three years were enormously stimulating; everything was new and exciting. It was a huge thrill. The company prospered and I had a big Thunderbird I drove around, and I started playing golf. It was really nice. For a couple of years I had the L-1 visa, but then we worked on getting a green card for me, and a few years later I received that. I have had that since. Now I sit here in my house looking out over the valley thinking that I came here fifteen years ago with two suitcases on a three-month project.... It was mostly a question of me not going back.

Before I came here I thought my English was very good, but then it turned out that maybe it was not all that good. It was a bit difficult. I managed what I had to get done and I was able to communicate. But it was a lot of work. I had to think about it all the time and my head was very tired in the evenings. During those first years when I went out with a group of people and there was laughing and joking, things were pretty easy to understand, but not always. If I tried to say something myself, a quick joke that was not pronounced well enough for them to understand, it would just fall flat. Repartee, if it isn't quick enough, isn't funny at all. After two or three years I got beyond that, and was able to live with the language. I'd like to say that when you first arrive here you think you know English, when all you really know is tourist English. Of course, your school English might still be better than that of many other countries. In general I would say that a Swede speaks a great deal more English than a German or a Frenchman.

People don't realize the difference between being a tourist and really living here—when everything you do has to be done in that language, everything from the TV news to the waitress rattling off the special on the menu. At first these things flew way over my head.

When you are a Swede in the United States, you have an unambiguous identity. There is no question as to what you are, not like: "My great-grandmother was Swedish." No, you are definitely Swedish. It is also a pretty well-respected background to have—decent, easy-going, problem free. So people always paid attention. I never passed by unnoticed, but there was never anything negative about it. I never felt discriminated against, other than what is natural for being an outsider and not speaking the language fluently. On the contrary, people often became interested, almost so interested that it became tedious to talk about Sweden all the time. Everyone pretty much asks the same things. Some Americans ask about the cheeses and the clocks, and what they mean is *Switzerland*. But those who know that Sweden is located where it is, and has the climate it does, will ask: "So, Sweden, is it pretty cold up there?" And then, as a bachelor talking with other bachelors, the subject of Swedish girls would often come up, of course. Clichés! Others, who are a bit more curious and well-educated, are more likely to ask about taxes and the social system in general. So even if they don't know, they want to find out about it. When you tell them that there is a 25% sales tax, they are simply dumbfounded! Everybody reacts to that one. And most people believe, correctly perhaps, that Sweden is pretty socialistic in a general, undefined way and a bit semi-communistic sometimes. They probably don't have a really clear sense of how much of a market economy it has or not.

What most people have heard about is something like the Nobel Prizes, but I don't know if they are that impressed by them. They know that they exist. You don't meet very many who know much at all about Sweden. But those who have been there, and you do run into people like that, find Swedish nature very beautiful. And when you start telling them a little bit, they are always impressed that you can study for free at the university and that everybody is covered by universal health care. Those sound good. On the other hand they are flabbergasted when you tell them about taxes. Most Americans don't understand the Swedish balancing act. I think they are pretty impressed by what they know of Volvo and SAAB, that they are quality cars. They do know that. Technology has a good reputation. The same thing is true for Swedish design, furniture, Scandinavian furniture in general—we have stores like Dania and Scan Design here. People find that look modern and pretty, that is, if you like that style at all!

It is very easy to fit in here, and everything is always open. It is a very comfortable life. When it comes to food, you have to learn the names of things, what you like and don't like. Sometimes the vocabulary is different, but most things are pretty much the same; it is not exactly exotic. And once you have located the Scandinavian store, you can even buy some caviar too.

It's an easy-going lifestyle: you can drive a big car, play golf, buy a beer whenever you want, go to or socialize in bars that are simple and cheap and fun. In Sweden it is such a big deal to go out, and you only do it on the weekends. Here it can happen any day of the week. Americans easily strike up conversations with each other when they go out, but it does get a bit superficial. You don't exactly have profound conversations where you discuss politics and religion. But my greatest personal change probably already happened at Chalmers. That's where I learned to become more outgoing, where I bloomed, so to speak. What was most difficult for me was probably being a bachelor; weeknights got boring sometimes. But that would have been the case anywhere; it did not necessarily have anything to do with being in the United States. If you are tired of being single, you are tired of it wherever you are. I felt a bit lonesome after a while, once the first intense socializing had come to an end. I still spent a lot of time with the other Swedes, but none of my friends from Gothenburg lived in Oregon. So there were no old friends nearby, just these new people from work. Occasionally there was some socializing during the day, but in the evenings there would not always be something. It was difficult to go out in the evening and just start a conversation with someone, because I did feel handicapped in terms of the language. I suppose I am not the kind of person who just goes to a bar and meets and picks up girls that easily. Some people can do that naturally; others can't. It is not always a question of nationality. Perhaps it was slightly more difficult for me to come here and not know how everything worked, and to have this accent. Occasionally it was an advantage, because it made me interesting, but usually it was just complicated because I could not make myself understood. That was especially true for the first years.

The Swedes I ran across in the United States I mostly met through work, and they were not very many. One Swede I worked with disappeared in a small airplane in the Bermuda Triangle! During my first year here our company was a subsidiary and we did not have a particularly active communication with Sweden. I worked as a consultant, and in the companies where I worked there were no Swedes. So I met Americans. After a while the wife of another Swede in the company got to know other Swedish women, and I began to meet these families at various parties around here, so I got to know more Swedes than just the ones I worked with.

Through a friend who was married to someone who worked for Oregon Software, I met my wife. She is from Ontario, Oregon, near the Idaho border. She had attended a folk high school in Denmark for a year and become interested in Scandinavia. She was actually a member of a Danish organization when she heard about this Swede. It was at a gathering at a Swedish couple's home that we met. We had coffee together that first time, and then there was a dinner that we both went to. We continued seeing each other after that. That was in 1988, but it took a while before we started living together. We got married in Sweden; it was in *Bönans Kapell* outside Gävle. It is located right in the middle of Bönan, opposite the restaurant there. It is just a small chapel. This was in June, around midsummer. My wife's parents were unable to come. We combined the wedding with a honeymoon trip and were gone for four weeks. Later that summer we visited her parents. There was no church ceremony or anything, just an American get-together for her relatives. That was in 1990.

I guess my view of the United States has changed. I had these impressions from the films and the television series I had seen in my early years, before I had come here. Most of what you see in films and on television comes from detective series set in major metropolitan areas. What you realize when you have lived here for a while is that there are so many ordinary weekdays here too, regular workdays that are not much different from anywhere else. You go to work, come home, eat dinner, watch some television, then go to bed. It is nothing special. There is such a multitude of everything here that it is hard to generalize. You can say: Americans are noisy and loud, but then I know quite a few who are quiet and modest too. You can't say that everyone is a certain way. Most people I know something about have more or less the same kind of job, or a similar background, and live their daily lives somewhat like I do. But then there are large groups of people who live in trailers doing odd jobs—a completely different world. In this society, there are really big differences between different groups.

I don't know that coming to the United States was a great shock. It might be a question of me not having such great illusions, or that I simply did not give it much thought. I have learned a few new things, but that does not mean that I had the opposite opinion before. Maybe I did not have a particular opinion at all. But you do develop a point of view. Take the health care issue for example. I think it is stupid and impractical that it is tied to your place of employment. You have your insurance, but it varies depending on where you work. It is the employer who pays for health insurance, not people's taxes. In Sweden you can change jobs and nothing happens with your health insurance. But that's not the way it is here. I had never thought that it could be that way before. I think it is a pretty stupid system where you have to think about this if you are going to change jobs—not to mention all those who don't have a job. I mean all those who are in a tough spot. I have seen this now, and realize that it really can be rough; you can end up hurting if you have some really bad luck. There are always those who are lazy and apathetic and cause themselves grief—that group always exists—but even ordinary people with the best intentions can still get into a jam if they are struck by a chain of events with a very unfortunate outcome. I realize now that this can actually happen. It is somewhat frightening.

I do believe that the economic possibilities are better in the United States. I am an engineer with an ordinary salary. I am not self-employed, but everyone I talk to in Sweden says that it would be considerably more difficult if I lived—depending on where, of course—in a house in a small Swedish city. My wife would have to work in order to make ends meet; otherwise, we would be taxed to death. And it would not be that easy to just come and quickly find a worthwhile job for my wife. But I don't have a substantial experience of how it was in Sweden. I have friends in Sweden, entrepreneurs who have done quite well, but they don't get really wealthy. Then you have to get into big business. One thing that they have also said is that there are a lot of small companies in Sweden, and a few very big ones, such as Ericsson,* for example. In between, there are not many that have grown larger, expanded beyond the small company category, but have not reached the group of large multi-nationals either. It is difficult to grow.

Swedish attitudes are, I suppose, part of the equation in my decision to live in the United States. Sometimes when I visit Sweden, I get a bit irritated about this "Swedishness," that everything should be just so. Just take playing golf as

---

* Ericsson quickly grew into Sweden's largest telecommunications company. Today it is known as Sony-Ericsson and is a global mobile phone technology company.

an example—they have millions of tiny little rules that they are dead serious about, instead of just playing to have some fun. They take it so seriously! When you play, there is always some little rule, for example, that if you happen to touch the ball, it will count as a stroke. In general, Swedes do things meticulously according to the rules. If you go out and play golf on a Saturday with your friends here—sure, we try to do it right, but it is not pedantic like that.

The Swedes who live in the United States are a bit more relaxed, I think. Those who remain here are normally not the socialist types, because it is much more difficult to live here if you have the attitude that society is there to take care of you. In general, they are probably pretty ambitious individuals who would like to do something on their own.

I have had some visitors who come with their Swedish comments about quality regarding everything, and "This is not how we do it in Sweden. We do it the right way. Things are done the wrong way here." Most of us have perhaps reacted that way initially too, but I am now at the point where I can say: "OK. It doesn't have to be done this way, it can be done that way also. That works too." Take this thing about quality for example: you can buy really cheap stuff here, and you know that it won't last very long, but you may only want it for a while. If you have not paid very much for it, well, then you buy another one when it breaks. But in Sweden it is supposed to be just right, high quality, and a lot of money upfront.

My parents never said: "No, don't move there!" Well, my mother is always nervous about most things and said: "Be careful now!" But they were happy for me that I got the opportunity to come here and see the United States.

And my first two trips here were just that—visits. But it is difficult to have family left in Sweden because it is so far away. I would like to see my children get to know my parents, of course, and my cousins' children who are of the same age, and all the others. My parents find the journey to Oregon tiresome, but they still come. It does not get easier with age, on the contrary, they could lose their energy to travel. During the last four or five years they have come here if we have not gone to Sweden. I call Sweden once a week, my parents mostly. They have a computer and we send emails back and forth. Occasionally I will call one of my old friends. That's somewhat sporadic. We had just a few visits from Swedish friends and acquaintances. During these fifteen years there are three or four—maybe five— who have come at different times. Then there has been the occasional visit from a mutual friend through work.

The last time we were in Sweden was for Midsummer celebrations.[†] I guess it wasn't a formal family reunion, more of an extended family gathering, but it was held at my uncle's cabin outside Gävle and all the relatives were there. And then, because my mother's relatives also live in Gävle, we met them as well, but not at the same event. That was a lot of relatives all at once. An extended family reunion was held on a family farm called Wikegård a couple of years ago, maybe five years ago, but I lived here then. It was at midsummer and I had not planned my vacation for that time, which was a pity, because I would really have liked to have gone to that. If it had been a question of going there for a weekend, I would have done it! One thing

---

† The midsummer celebrations in Sweden are always held on the Friday closest to the summer solstice. It is a major Swedish holiday.

I really regret—and I have to kick myself for it—was not attending the 50th anniversary of the Alliance Orchestra and the annual Chalmers Student Farce in Gothenburg. The reason was that we were in the process of buying this house, and there was a lot of back and forth going on and papers to sign. And then my wife went on a three-week trip with her mother just prior to it, and my parents were due to come here the week after these events in Sweden. Everything happened within just a few months, and I could have bought a cheap ticket if I had ordered it in January, but I did not dare.

Once I actually did go back to Gothenburg. When I had been here two or three years, I returned for the 35th anniversary. I had a ball. But this last event was a cut above that, because it was 50 years. That hurts. Sometimes, when I realize I miss things like that because it gets too complicated to travel, I wonder: *Why did I end up here?* That's when I miss my roots, when I feel pulled-up with my roots. If there had been a Concorde flight, Portland directly to Gothenburg, everything would have worked itself out—especially if it had been cheap too! Portland is located in the margin: there are no direct flights to Europe, you have to change planes, it is complicated, and takes a fair amount of time.

Growing up, I was close to both my maternal and paternal grandparents, and my children don't have that here. Early on Christmas Eve we always went to my maternal grandparents first, or to my mother's family, and later in the evening to my father's family. And we had the next morning to ourselves. So there were three opportunities for Christmas presents when I was a child. It was wonderful. We don't have that here; it is only us. My wife's parents—well, she actually only has her mother left now—lives far away, six hours by car. She flies over for a visit sometimes, but in general, family holidays in Oregon are very different.

I try to speak Swedish to my children. It went well initially. During the early years my daughter could speak fairly decent Swedish. But now that she is older and has learned more—she has been in kindergarten for a year—during the days she learns so much more English than Swedish. If I speak Swedish to her now, with the kind of conversations she has at this age, she does not understand enough. And my son, unfortunately, has even less Swedish. Partly, it has to do with me too. I relax, and it becomes so much easier to say it in English so that they will understand. Sometimes I find myself speaking Swedish and my son will say: "Don't talk in Swedish!" When my parents come, things improve because they get a real workout in Swedish. But the children don't have the same vocabulary in Swedish that they do in English. My wife and I speak English with each other, and in a larger group of Swedes she understands a fair amount, but not everything: not when it gets too complicated, not when people talk about unusual subjects, not when it goes too fast, not when there are too many dialects. As it turns out, she is actually capable of saying a fair amount. It always surprises me how much she really knows.

I am a member of SHF, Scandinavian Heritage Foundation. Ross Fogelquist was a leading figure there—well, he is still active there—but he is not the President any longer. He is in the process of donating some of his land on which a living museum is to be built. SHF also arranges some Scandinavian events and festivities. These

Swedish organizations are complicated, spread out, and fragmented. I can't understand why it should be so difficult for us Swedes to get together! I think it sounds like a good idea for the Swedes to obtain a building or a space to meet in. But it should be real, actively Swedish, and Swedish has to be spoken. Perhaps it would be unfortunate to divide the community with yet another organization .... And how many of one's ideas are actually ever realized? It is easy to sit here and say that it would be great. We live out here in a suburb, but if such a gathering place would be located in NW Portland, for example, it would be too far for an evening visit. And if it would be located on Portland's east side, well, then I would hardly ever go there. Then there are others who live on the east side, and they would say the same thing if it would be located out here, although NW Portland would be a pretty good compromise for most people. But what I like best is actually the Swedish School in Portland. I think it has been very good, because the children get to experience Lucia and things like that. I also think that this is the most fun group to be with, because they are my age and they all have children. So I have decided to get involved there a little bit. To the extent I am able. Members of the other groups, well, they are a bit older. Rather too old. And there are not too many active Swedes.

During my first years in the United States, when speaking English was still a chore, I thought it was really nice to be able to relax and speak Swedish and not have to think about how to say something, you know, just say it. Be able to tell a joke. Now my English is good enough that this is no longer as important, and I can express myself pretty freely in English. There are no language limitations. Well, sometimes there are! It is still not like my native language. There can be complications like that in Swedish too, when you get yourself tangled up. I don't speak Swedish every day, I really don't. But I still speak quite a lot, because I spend time with two Swedes and we like to play golf. And then I try to do a few things on my own with the kids. I read Swedish books, sometimes for the children, sometimes out of personal interest. For a while it was mostly for the children, so we have a bunch of Swedish children's books now. I read in Swedish relatively often. For example, I have read Herman Lindqvist's series on Swedish history, and Henning Mankell's crime novels. I have read all of Jan Guillou's books over here.‡ When I get one I read it, and when I'm done I have to wait until I get a chance to get a new one again!

I don't subscribe to any Swedish newspapers or magazines. I have found Swedish newspapers online and checked them out a little bit, but I don't read them regularly. I have found the news broadcast "*Dagens Eko*" on *Sveriges Radio* too, and I listen to that. It is pretty impressive that this is possible. We rent a foreign film occasionally, but it could just as well be French as Swedish. There are not that many Swedish movies available—I have never watched much Swedish film—what you can find are these old Bergman movies. What you can rent is limited. That's unfortunate, because renting movies is so easy. I think that these big chains really could carry more foreign films. I have gone to Portland's International Film Festival a couple of times to see Swedish movies, but not having a steady baby sitter makes going to the movies difficult in general.

---

‡ All three are very popular, contemporary Swedish authors.

I think the Swedes in Sweden are pretty much the same as they have always been, at least the older ones. The relatives and friends I meet have not changed very much. I know a lot of people who whine about the government, taxes and so on, but then, darn it, they vote for the Social Democrats anyway! I mean, most of them do. They don't dare change anything! The younger generation has maybe changed a little bit. Things have a more international feel now; it is a bit more open than it used to be. The Swedes are much more aware of the rest of Europe. A café serving beer outside is not that unusual anymore; things are more easy-going. Sweden seems to have become a bit more open and free. But on the other hand there are aspects that have become worse: violence that is more brutal, just more violence, and trouble in general. If I were to walk down a street in Stockholm late at night, I think I would feel less at ease than if I walked down Broadway here in Portland. Living here you know that there are certain areas where you never walk around at night, and maybe it is that way in Stockholm too, but it seems to me that this can happen anywhere in Stockholm and Gothenburg.

I think my view of Sweden has changed. When I lived there, I bought into this whole notion—the way you do it Sweden, that's *the* way to do it! Then, when you have been around and seen a few other things, you realize: *No, you don't have to do it that way; there are ten different ways to do it. They are just as good.* These Swedish standards for how things are to be done ... well, if you don't follow them you can still live with the results. You get perspective on things. In spite of everything, Sweden is something of a duck-pond. Swedes in Sweden think about Sweden as rather remarkable, that everybody listens to and hears

Sweden's voice in the world, the home of the Nobel Prizes and Ericsson …. There is always a great deal of talk about things that are pretty significant, but when you come out into the rest of the world, you wonder: *Sweden—now, where is that exactly?* My God, if the Swedes realized what a tiny little country it is in many ways! Sweden has no perspective on that.

My opinion is that Sweden should be a part of the European Union—if it works. I mean, Sweden ought to be part of Europe as a matter of principle. You hear these weird stories about rules for the curvature of cucumbers and things like that, but if they are true something is wrong with the EU, not with the fact that Sweden is a member of EU. If the EU is doing this, it has to be corrected. You can't isolate yourself; Sweden can't afford to be isolated. I like the fact that as a Swedish citizen—theoretically at least—I would be able to move to any of those countries and start working there. It is an attractive thought, even if it is never realized.

I have not seen any reason to become an American citizen. There have not been any clear advantages to it. Unless you do some tricks and cheat and not say anything, you are, at least theoretically, supposed to give up your Swedish citizenship if you become an American citizen. But that is risky. And furthermore, if you retain your Swedish citizenship, you at least have a significantly greater chance to move your family to Sweden, if that is what you want. If I become an American citizen, that's no longer possible. Then it is not easy to move back. The way the world is now, it is unfortunate that Sweden does not allow dual citizenship. We live in such an international world that it is both very petty and limiting to cling to nationality problems of this sort. Why not be generous? You pay taxes where you reside, whether you are a citizen or not. So that's what counts, really. So there could be some generosity with this whole citizenship issue.

Some really decide that this living in the United States, *this is it*. There is not going to be any moving back and they become citizens and so on. And then there are the rest of us, who don't do that.... In my case, and this is true for many people I know, emigrating had nothing to do with moving here out of necessity; it was an opportunity I took. Living in the United States was fun, exciting initially. Then life here became regular workdays too, but a very nice, enjoyable everyday life! Whether you have strong attachments to Swedish culture and family ties—or whether you don't—this probably influences your decision to break off contact. I say "break off contact," but I mean becoming a citizen and remaining here. If I could travel to Sweden for a weekend, practically speaking, I think I would be able to say: "This is it! I can live here, but I can go there any weekend I want." But I can't do that.

I suppose I am always thinking about moving back to Sweden. Well, I don't know how realistic it really is, especially when you consider your pension and taxes and everything else. The longer you live here, the more difficult it becomes. Sometimes I almost regret that I did not return at an earlier time when it was not that difficult. Before I bought that condo.... The children are a pretty powerful factor. For the children it is a question of traditions and language. If we don't move to Sweden, they will, of course, grow up as Americans and with that tradition. After all, I do live here and there is nothing wrong with that. That's what I have done for fifteen years now—wait and see. If my wife, for reason, disappeared out of my life, I think I would move back to Sweden. I think it would be something that triggered a change, since I have had these thoughts in my head. It would be such a drastic change in my life no matter what, that I probably would take the opportunity to make that change. I would not have any problems finding work in Sweden, unless I get too old, of course.

Feeling at home in the United States is a gradual process; it is not over yet! Of course, now that I have a family it is my home, but it still is not my true roots—they are still attached over there .... What is really complicated is this: IF I were to move back to Sweden, really break free and do it, it might not feel completely right either. I would definitely miss a great many things from here. I have become one of those people who do not have any country that I can call my real and true home!

VI

I Received the Best of Both Worlds

Carin (b. 1953)

Portland, Oregon, 1998

.

I first came to the United States in the summer of 1973, right after completing my teaching degree in Physical Education at the School of Sport and Health Sciences in Stockholm. I just wanted to try something different. A friend from Nyköping had worked as a nanny in Chicago, so I thought I should try being a nanny in Chicago, too. The family preferred someone my friend could personally recommend, and I wanted to be with a family that I knew something about. She had told me all about her experience. So that's what I did, illegally, just like all other nannies.

The family lived in a suburb of Chicago called Highland Park. I thought it was really exciting since I had ended up with a good family. They were young, only ten years older than me, two children, everything was just great. The girl went off to school and the boy was home quite a bit.

It was a Jewish family, but not orthodox Jewish. This was new to me because in Sweden I never even thought about whether someone was Jewish or not. They had just moved into a new house and were well off—upper middle class, I would guess. It was easy working for them. They didn't look down on me at all as a nanny—I was more like another member of the family. They took me everywhere they went. During the summer we went to St. Louis, and I went skiing with them in Colorado at Christmas time.

I drove the girl to her school, so I had to get a driver's license. The boy sometimes went to a part-time preschool, and I took him there and back home again. I did a fair amount of household work: laundry, vacuuming, general cleaning up. It had to be done quite thoroughly. The woman was a housewife and prepared a lot of the meals. I worked alongside her. I didn't have complete responsibility, except for making lunches and so on. They had a healthy lifestyle, ate a lot of fruit and salads, and in many ways it was like Swedish food. Nothing was particularly special or traditional. The taste of *grape jelly* is one of my strongest memories from that year because I had never tasted it before. I went swimming with the children over the summer and we did some bike riding. In Sweden, people rode their bikes to work, parking them at the railroad station or at the school. It occurred to me that riding a bicycle in the United States was an activity for which you needed special equipment.

Other people found me interesting because I was Swedish. In those days you also heard a lot of comments about Swedish girls being open to *free sex*. The comments weren't directed at me personally but it was always, "In Sweden, you know, everybody...." It was as if everyone immediately thought of the movies "*I Am Curious (Yellow)*" and "*I Am Curious (Blue).*"

There were four or five of us Swedish *au pair* girls who hung out together. It's amazing how you always find out about each other. Because one family knew about another family with an *au pair*, they helped track down phone numbers so that we could call each other. So we immediately became friends. We lived about 40 minutes apart, but my family had a car that I could borrow. It was a huge difference to come to a place where you had to drive a car everywhere you went. I had never had a car before. Nyköping was so small that you could bike, walk, or take the bus.

Chicago has a completely different climate: hot in the summer and cold in the winter. The year I was there was a year for cicadas, insects with barbed legs flying around, getting stuck in your clothes. It was disgusting. I didn't go outside for three or four weeks. Every morning you had to sweep away dead cicadas on the front porch. They only live for one day. Every seventeenth year they appear there.

In Sweden there are maybe two kinds of cornflakes; here there were twenty-seven different kinds to choose from. Many things are super-sized in America: huge super markets, really big houses, big yards, two or three cars per family, enormous cars. My family had a gigantic American station wagon as their family car, and this was during the energy crisis. They cut down a little bit on their driving I suppose, but not that much. Back in Sweden, our family wasn't the first one to own a TV, so we had to go to our neighbors to watch. Here I could have my own TV in my bedroom! I thought I had it made. Later on it became too much because I put on thirty pounds, and I felt that I needed to do something else besides just hang out there. So

I didn't stay the whole year. The family was not too happy about me leaving early, but it turned out OK. Staying in the United States to do something else was not even an option, because it was difficult to get a permanent visa. I just had a tourist visa. So I came back home in February of 1974.

I really didn't see Sweden with new eyes when I came home that time—not the way I do now. I was too young for that sort thing and had been away for such a short time. Any change was more on a personal level. My host family was totally American, so they were not able to discuss things like that. But they were curious about Sweden and wanted to learn more. They had taken me along to Andersonville, the old Swedish neighborhood in Chicago, and bought crayfish. I met the family once when they came to Sweden for a visit, but by that time I had already moved to the United States. We met in Stockholm. We are not in touch with each other anymore.

I went back to Nyköping. I was not brave enough to try moving somewhere else. I got my first job substitute teaching for a male Physical Education teacher at a school in Nyköping. I was twenty-one and I was instructing boys in junior high in physical education. Just imagine!

"Teacher, can we play soccer today?"

"But we really ought to do some folk dancing and gymnastics . . ."

"Great, we'll do soccer!"

My stint as a substitute lasted for three months; it was actually rather stressful. However, I did manage to lose those thirty pounds in four weeks simply by bicycling back and forth to work.

I worked as a teacher from 1974 to 1980, when I began

to wonder if it was good for me to be a teacher. I'm a Type A personality and put high demands on myself. Everything has to be perfect. Along with another colleague, I attended the Mullsjö Seminars four summers in a row. They were held at Mullsjö in the province of Småland. These seminars derived some of their inspiration from the United States. John Steinberg, an American educator who lived in Örebro, had started it. He had written several books on assessment and teaching methods. Educators from the United States came over to Sweden so that we wouldn't have to travel there—something we couldn't afford. Finally I decided to switch to something else and applied both to medical school and to the physical therapy program. I was accepted into both, except that for the pre-med program I would have to add a lot of subjects which I hadn't studied in high school. So I started studying again, but one day, in the middle of a math class, someone came in and told me there was an opening for me in the physical therapy program. I had to make a decision that same day. I felt like it was the hand of Fate. Alright—it was like *I guess that's what I am supposed to do*. My mother had always claimed that being a physical therapist was very international. You can do that kind of work all over the world. I heard my mother's dreams when she said that. So I moved to Stockholm and enrolled in the physical therapy program at the Karolinska Institute, the medical university. It took two and half years and was a total break from my life in Nyköping. I finished after the fall semester in 1984. I felt like, *phew, now I need a break*! I just wanted to travel somewhere and ended up in Eugene, Oregon.

What had happened was that my brother had been an exchange student in Eugene in 1972 – 73. He went through the last year of high school there. He had lived in a student apartment, but also had a host family to visit on weekends and holidays. I was in touch with that family because we had visited them briefly in the summer of 1983. The mother was from Oregon, but her grandmother had been born in Sweden. The father was born in Denmark and had come over when he was thirteen. He could still speak Danish. They were sweet people and had always said that we were welcome to stay with them. *Wonderful,* I thought. *I'll go visit.* When I arrived in Eugene, I discovered that physical therapists were in demand. I thought maybe that was worthwhile looking into. Everyone said, "Oh, you have studied in Sweden; they have such good physical therapy programs there!" When I heard that, I was really glad to have such a highly respected education. I could have had a job the very next day—at five different clinics in Eugene! So I went to the local INS office and they were very friendly. They were very helpful and showed me a paragraph stating that physical therapists were number one of all the professions they allowed into America. So I filled out my immigration papers and sent them in. Then I went back home to Stockholm and started working at a hospital in Norrtälje.

I couldn't get any information on the status of my application. It was a process that would take about a year. I spent all year preparing myself. I knew I was eventually going to move. I was bound and determined to do it. No one could stop me; that's how it felt. However, I thought I was only going to be away for a few years, like an adventure, to see if I could do it. That's how I handle many things in life. I want to know if I can do it. I was raised with a can-do attitude and that you should work hard. So, I was trying to learn something new. It is much more important to know how much you like something, or how you feel, when you are applying yourself to something.

In January, 1986, I got a call from the American Embassy saying that it was my turn. I was required to visit a doctor, answer questions, sign papers, get fingerprinted. All very official. And you had to swear that you had never been part of anything Anti-American. *Oh, God,* I thought, *I had been a protester in 1968 against the War in Vietnam wearing an FNL button.** I wondered if they had discovered that I had overstayed my visa eight months in Chicago, even though I was not supposed to do that. It was a little scary. I was pretty sure they had all my records and could dig up something from the past. I arrived in Seattle with my huge x-ray photos of my lungs in a yellow, twenty-by-twenty inch envelope because they had to be delivered to the immigration officials in person. At the airport there was no trouble at all, and for the most part they were very friendly.

Between 1974 and 1980 I had been in two long-term relationships, but I never got engaged to be married. Back at that seminar at Mullsjö, I met a man ten years older than me, and I was really attracted to him. He was an educator, very nice, very cool, and I looked up to him. But it was a very complex, unbalanced relationship. When I left for Eugene, I also left all that behind me. We had broken up. It was also a kind of escape, but I didn't cut all my ties to Sweden. I hadn't sold my apartment in Stockholm, so it was waiting there in Vasastan with all my stuff. I rented it to

---

* The Swedish anti-war movement used the abbreviation of the French *Front National pour la Libération du Sud Viêt Nam.*

someone. So I only took two suitcases with me, and bought everything new here—a bookshelf, kitchen table, a sofa.

I had a job waiting for me in Eugene. The family there didn't have to sponsor me anymore. They offered to do that, but I wanted to start from scratch on my own. I discovered that it wasn't easy to get car insurance. No one knew anything about me; I had no driving record in the United States. That I was a responsible person didn't count at all. That was almost like an insult: Here I was, an honorable Swede, having driven a car since I was eighteen without a single accident. Then, on top of that, they sort of insinuated that I would not even be allowed to buy a car. And I could not get a home phone line unless I had references in the United States. So my local family did help me out with these issues. I found myself an apartment and started working for a physical therapist, a young woman who had just opened her own practice. I was her first employee. We had our own little business, but we rented space in a clinic for sports injuries, so there were lots of different therapists there. The owner and I became very good friends, a friendship that has lasted to this day.

Initially, I did my job with a temporary license. You can't get a work permit as a physical therapist until the US Board of Physical Therapists has approved your education, which seemed excessively bureaucratic to me—as if *they* could figure out if my education was good or not. I had to send a pile of their papers to the Department of Immigration. Fortunately, I didn't have to go back to school. Some people have to, and I don't really know why, but I think it must have been because I had two degrees. I also had to prepare for the Oregon license test. I couldn't get that license in Sweden. It was a gigantic test which was offered twice a year, an all-day-long affair, and I wasn't used to filling in little circles on a computer sheet with a number-2 lead pencil, and it was a multiple-choice test. That's when I realized how different my education had been. I discovered that Sweden was ten years ahead in my field. I still think that Sweden is more advanced in many areas: physical therapy, general treatment, job definition, and job reputation—all that stuff. We had worked mostly with ergonomics, and here they didn't even know how to spell the word! I don't want to sound condescending. It's just a developmental matter, and it might be a cultural thing, too.

As a physical therapist in Sweden, you had a much more equal standing with the doctors than you do here. In Sweden doctors and therapists often worked side by side, except perhaps some of the older doctors. There was a lot more teamwork in Sweden. Perhaps that isn't as true today in Sweden, but at that time it was emphasized. As a female physical therapist in the US, I was a rung lower than a male therapist, who himself was three rungs lower than the doctors. I especially noticed this when I took my second job at a hospital in Portland. Then I really appreciated that I was born and raised in Sweden where equality between the sexes is stressed. Eventually I couldn't stay with that job. As a Swedish woman, I really experienced the difference. And I am sad that my own daughter won't experience this equality because she could use a little more self-esteem. I think this is still something of a problem here.

I felt very strongly that I emigrated, that I moved. It was definitive. I think my family thought it was exciting. My brother had already been to the United States. My mother in particular, thought it was sad that I would be so far away, but at the same time she admitted that she had always encouraged me to choose a profession in which I would have the opportunity to travel. So there were pros and cons. And they had a whole year to adjust to the idea of my move. I don't think I really thought I'd live in the US forever. Because I realized that I had the opportunity, I wanted to do something new. Emotionally I had made the move to the US, but by leaving all my physical things behind, I could always go back home again. From an emotional point of view, it was a way to break free, because I had never really broken free from Nyköping, the town of my childhood and youth. I had never been totally on my own. This was my chance to leave it all behind because both my parents had been very strong influences. Going through with it, I think I grew up.

For me it was very exciting to move away from Sweden and my parents. That's how far I had to move! My family in Eugene was younger than my parents, a bit more easy-going, open, friendly, cheerful, and easier to talk with. They were not weighed down with all that Swedish "Don't dare stand out from the crowd," all those duties and obligations, *jantelagen*,† and everything that comes with it. The American family didn't have all that, and it was very liberating to discover that things didn't have to be so gloomy and burdensome, that it was alright to take it easy, to do the things you wanted. Here, in the United States, you are actually allowed to be proud of your ability

---

† *Jantelagen*, or Jante's Law, refers to a pattern of group behavior towards individuals within Scandinavian communities, which negatively portrays and criticizes success and achievement as unworthy and inappropriate. The term refers to a snide, jealous, and narrow mentality which refuses to acknowledge individual effort and places all emphasis on the collective, while punishing those who stand out as achievers.

to accomplish certain things. For me, Eugene was a sunny, sunny town. The sunlight really appeared to be quite different here. Even the light we have right now. It is never the same as it used to be at home in Sweden. I was never as healthy there as I have been here in America.

In Sweden, I had been going out with a man. We both knew that I was about to leave but we hadn't made things clear. He thought it was a great idea when he decided to follow me here. He sold all his stuff and came along. It was hard on me because eventually I had to tell him that that I hadn't planned on that. He arrived here and moved in with me just as I started working at my new job. He was in the merchant marine and thought this was great, because he gotten on a regular shipping route to Portland. So he stayed with me for two months before he went to sea again. He was twelve years younger, a very charming guy from the province of Skåne, but was not what I had in mind. We had kept writing to each other, but I hadn't realized he was getting so serious.

Another thing that was annoying about being Swedish was the issue of "free sex." That stereotype of Swedish women was still current in the United States, even twelve or thirteen years after I had been in Chicago. Of course, I was older, but Americans who don't know that much about Sweden have heard of that stereotype. Even people who were not like that felt that it was necessary to make that comment—just to get it out in the open. Americans really know very little about Sweden. It still happens to me over and over again that someone says: "Oh you're from Switzerland!" I'm still surprised by that, even from people who should know better.

A little later, through my boss, I met the man who

would become my husband. The following summer, in June, we got married in Sweden. Our daughter arrived in 1988. I had never been married before. If we had lived in Sweden, I'm not so sure we would have gotten married, but here it was expected. Living together would have been fine with me, and I think my husband could have done that too. He had been living with another woman for sixteen years before we met. He's probably pretty radical for an American. If he had not been, he says, he would never have been able to live together with me. When push comes to shove, I am still very Swedish. Despite my appreciation for Americans being so positive, cheerful, and easy-going, I can always throw in some criticism against the way it is here.

When my daughter was born, it was very important to me that we follow the recommendations from the National Swedish Board of Health and Welfare. To me, it was a question of feeling secure. I had faith in the fact that Sweden, from the 1940's on, had done enough research to arrive at recommendations that were pretty reasonable. It was reassuring for me to follow them, especially when doctors in the United States said things that were completely different. I was not about to go along with all the nonsense they did here. I told my obstetrician that too: "No Caesarian section for me! We don't do that in Sweden." I had read up on that. In the United States 28 percent of the births are by C-sections, but in Sweden it's only three to five percent. It was also a question of security to be able to trust the recommendations from the National Board of Health and Welfare in matters such as when to start feeding babies cereal and whether they should sleep on their stomachs or backs. Now, with more maturity, I can take a more critical view, look back and question certain things, but back then, those recommendations were a big deal to me.

My daughter's first language was Swedish. I still only speak Swedish with her. I think being bilingual has worked really well for us. My husband has never perceived it as a threat. He doesn't speak Swedish fluently but he can still make himself understood. We sit around the dinner table and chatter away in Swedish and my husband can follow along. He understands everything; he just doesn't speak Swedish himself. He sticks to English, and sometimes we switch into English. We don't have a clearly established rule that says, "When Daddy is around, we must always speak English."

I have tried to provide my daughter with as much Swedish culture as possible. We have also hired Swedish *au pairs*, not so much for the language benefits, but as role models for the way Swedes behave—the way you act when you come directly from Sweden. For example, that nakedness is natural. My husband, fortunately, is very open to all this in spite of his Catholic upbringing. He is half Irish and half Czech. His mother is very Catholic, carries a rosary, and must go to Mass every Sunday. My husband was married once before and, therefore, cannot remain in the Church any longer.

During the first few years I thought that we would probably be able to move back to Sweden at some point. Later on I began to realize it wouldn't happen because my husband wasn't prepared to do it. He was not willing to give up everything we had over here, break away, and move into the unknown. He was taking Swedish classes and has always had a very positive view of Sweden, and a desire to learn things about Sweden. He has never said anything negative about it, but he has a hard time with moving in general. Changes are difficult for him to cope with. But I didn't know that because I didn't know him that well. It took me about a year before it occurred to me: *Nope! I won't be able to take him along with me to Sweden. Not even to try it out.* He was happy to come to Sweden to get married, but he has a pretty strong sense of being the breadwinner of the family, far more than I would insist on. I am very independent and have always taken care of myself. He got more conservative after having been quite radical when he first moved out to the west coast and became something of a hippie. . . .

I was quite depressed during this time because I might not be able to move back home to Sweden. If someone just mentioned Sweden, I sometimes started to cry. That was a much greater loss than my actual move away from Sweden. In some way it felt like I couldn't move back now because I had a family of my own. That was the first time I felt I was here against my will. I had been here of my own free will the whole time. So for several years I felt caged in, and that feeling of grief and homesickness lingered for quite some time.

I longed to go back to Sweden very much. And I got quite sad. It was a very difficult time for my husband and me. I put a lot of pressure on him, which was certainly quite cruel of me. Still, I only went home about once a year. During this time I sold my apartment in Stockholm and brought my things over in a container. That was in 1990. All my furniture, all my books, and belongings arrived from Sweden. I brought my life over here and felt sort of whole again. But it was difficult for my parents, I think, because it was a definitive move. Yet I still said: "Well, you shouldn't think I really want to stay in the United States that much, but the way things are, I have to." It probably took me ten years to feel at home here. Instead, I tried to do everything possible to make myself comfortable here, but it wasn't so easy to just decide that.

The Swedish coffee gatherings started in the back yard of a Swedish woman here in Portland. A few of the older ladies were part of it and we started by sending out a list. It was a very short list at the time. This went on for a few years and was very important to me. I also belong to the organization called New Sweden,[‡] but that is mostly for getting information. I think it was last year that I realized they were not Swedish. They don't speak Swedish at the meetings. They only speak English. They are Swedish-Americans, and that is not the same thing. There is nothing wrong with them: it's just that they live with these old traditions, or experience the Swedish traditions in a Swedish-American way. I don't feel at home there. They are too antiquated. On the other hand, in spite of that, I have still said, "Yes, I will help out or pay the membership fee because I do want to support them somehow." I haven't had the nerve to say, "No, I'll pass on that." Take folk dancing, for example. My daughter is a member of the dance group supported by Swedish Society Linnea. In this situation you have to make up your mind: you're either OK with the way it is, or you choose not belong to it. At the same time, I am really moved when I see those 85-year-olds enjoying a Lucia pageant—even though it may not

---

‡ The full name of this Portland organization is *New Sweden Cultural Heritage Society of Oregon and SW Washington.*

be done entirely in the Swedish way. It's the same when it comes to the Christmas party they put together—there are mostly older people there, too. There is hardly anyone from our generation anyway, and the children perform for them. I think it means a great deal to them. So I think it is important that some of these organizations continue. At the same time I also wish they could feel more comfortable about us doing a few more Swedish things.

I would like to belong to a group where I felt at home. I enjoy the Swedish coffee gatherings, but sometimes they're not at the top of my list. Actually, I have not put a priority on it for several years. I go maybe twice a year; in the past I went every month. It is an informal gathering where everyone speaks Swedish, and I like the interaction with the present-day Swedes there. I also belong to the Swedish School and I am almost more involved there than in the coffee gatherings. I think there should be more activities for the adults, though. We aren't very good at organizing ourselves. I think there is room for improvement in the community of present-day Swedes. But things are beginning to happen because there is a large group of young people who put on a Christmas party. That means a lot to me. And on the 18th of December there was a church service in Swedish and a choir that sang Christmas carols in Swedish. It was the best Christmas celebration I have ever been to—very much like it is in Sweden. I do feel, however, that I still belong to the Swedish State Church. I think that is because we were married by a Swedish minister, and that my brother was married by the same minister the year after, and that my daughter was baptized in Sweden.

I feel that my Swedish identity is part of my DNA. At any moment, images can surface of what it is like to sit on a jetty at five o'clock on a July morning in the Swedish archipelago, or tramp around in the woods looking for mushrooms. And even though I am not from Northern Sweden, there's a song about the train that goes there, *Norrlandspilen*. It is about an early Tuesday morning in November, very early, about his cold and lonesome train passing through the huge, open vistas of the North, about the atmosphere in the houses when one has to go outside in the morning. One can feel how cold and dark it is, and I know exactly how it is because I was often up there visiting my father when he was living in Norrland. It's so typically Swedish for me; just thinking about it can make me cry. Such feelings and moods will always be deeply etched in my mind, and I still want to experience them, but I don't have an overwhelming desire to move back to Sweden or become Swedish again in today's Sweden. It is not just cowardice on my part; it also has to do with how much I have changed, or how both have changed.

Both Sweden and I have been transformed. I don't feel any desire to return. Instead, I could think of moving to Denmark perhaps, or Norway. Finland, I could live on the Finnish west coast! In this context I think of myself as a Scandinavian. I am Swedish after all, even my way of thinking is Swedish, but I do not really want to return to that. I don't want to go back to that grumpy, whining, and complaining Sweden. I feel some distance from it, and even a bit alienated to the way it has become now. We joke about it here sometimes, and when I call Sweden, I sometimes joke about it with friends. I try to laugh at the way I have changed.

Then you also begin thinking about retirement. The future. And when I think about that, I don't want to retire here. I have a very strong feeling about that: I do NOT want to die here! So while I have come to an acceptance of the fact that I live here and have created a job that I like, I still know that I could move away tomorrow. My happiness does not depend on whether I get to live here or in Sweden. I could break away tomorrow—well, I might think about it a little bit and plan a little better. I might not move to Africa or to Indonesia, but move somewhere if I had to or wanted to. My happiness no longer depends on what country I live in. It does not depend on what city I live in. Not in what part of the city it is. Not where I work. Not even in what house I live. Now I have that feeling of security within myself. So I have become a "globe liver," not a globetrotter.

The longer I live in the United States, the more I notice what the differences are, so my view of it has changed. Initially I thought that a lot was organized the way it was in Sweden. Now my view of this has changed. I see America more like a quilt of many different countries now. It is not a single country where everything is the same—definitely not. It is almost more different than Europe. I don't think you have that feeling when you live in Sweden—then everything in America appears the same. My mother is always so surprised when I say: "Well, but that's not the way it is in Oregon!" For example, take one of these standard things in Sweden: a regulator on the hot water so that you can't scald yourself. In Sweden, they probably believe that we have that too, because it is such an obvious safety item. If you want to buy that valve here, you have to go to a store and special order it, then have a new installation done. And eight out of ten American plumbers would not know what you were talking about. Many Swedes might look up to America, think that all new things come from here, and take for granted that it is like that here. But that's not the way it is! We still have lamps in the United States that you turn on by pulling a string.

Now I will serve up a prejudice. The longer I live in America, the more I have discovered how little people actually know about the things they do. This might be something "super-Swedish" in me too, but my husband usually agrees with me. For example, I am completely surprised that they allow people to call themselves *tilers*. These trade people have not been to a trade school, and they have not worked as an apprentice for two years in a tiling business, and they have not done this or that. Here it is possible to say almost anything, and people do it too. I understand now that as soon as someone says something, you always have to check up on them and question what they say. It took a while for me to realize this, because I had this assumption of Swedish standards for everything. If you have a Swedish certificate or diploma, it shows that you have actually done what it says. You don't have to question it. It is not a mail order diploma someone has just bought. In Sweden, when you call an electrician, you take for granted that the electrician knows the rules and does the job in a satisfactory manner. But here you really have to make sure that someone has not just put "Electrician" on his business card this week.

I have a brother in the United States. That is good. He is contemplating becoming an American citizen because he works on various high security projects, and he can't work on some of them because he is not an American citizen. When we had a conversation about having to become an American citizen for some reason, I said that if we did it together, it might feel easier. If it would be possible to have dual citizenship, I might consider it. Otherwise I would not—with a clear conscience—be able to sing the American national anthem or swear the "Pledge of Allegiance." To me that would feel so wrong. But I would do it, if I had to, for the sake of my daughter.

We have bought a house here together with my mom. It is just two blocks away. She is not planning to live here all the time—that's not what she wants—but she would like to come and go as she pleases. And that is okay. My mother does not want to leave Sweden. It is fortunate that she is able to travel, but there might also come a day when she can't. She has spent a lot of time here. Some years she has been here twice and stayed for a month or two. And now it will be easier for her to visit my brother. Or he can come here for a long weekend. My mom has been here for many Christmas holidays, and my brother has come here to celebrate Swedish Christmas. My mother understands television English and that kind of thing, except a handful of words, perhaps. She converses in English with my husband and she is a bit shy, typically Swedish, when she is out in public. She actually has friends her own age here in Portland. She visits them when she comes here and they have visited her in Sweden. She knows how to drive, but she has never driven here. But now she has said that she will start practicing and drive around here. She definitely does not want to move here permanently, but on the other hand she has sometimes thought about moving a few things over. If she were to become sick, we know that she would be able to be here, close by, and we would be able to help her.

There is one really American phenomena that I can't relate to at all, and that is "the American Mom," a woman who does not have an active, vocational identity of her own, but only lives for and through her children. She exists for them, packs their lunches, drives them places, picks them up, lives for their successes. This is a bit difficult for me. I don't know if they exist in the same way in Sweden, but maybe I am just kidding myself. But there, you at least have a job, and even if you stay home with the children, it is for some reason still not the same. You don't give up as much of yourself. When you bring up "the image of Mom" in the United States, you have to let go of everything else, because then you have to show gratefulness to your mother. On Mother's Day it is almost okay to play hooky from work! You are supposed to be a good son or daughter. I don't know if it has to do with this self-sacrificing mother's role when you grew up, that you still pay tribute to it. The role of the mother is a bit different here—glorified in some way.

I think Americans view Swedes as ... not as spoiled perhaps, but that they have so much. When I went back to Sweden five years ago, I could say: "Oh my God, you don't know how good you have it here in Sweden." In those days you could basically be on maternity leave for as long as you wanted, or on paid sick leave. Sometimes I also think that Americans might believe that Swedes, or Sweden as a nation, is something of a know-it-all, that it gets involved a bit too much, has opinions. But then it has to be Americans who stay really informed. Just think of all the people who don't even know where Sweden is! But I think that there are more people in America who have a positive opinion of Sweden, or are impressed by something, than there are people who criticize it. I think that many academic and business people, if they travel to Europe, learn things about Sweden.

When I look at the Swedes who have come to the United States during the last couple of years, I think they are people who might be here to help themselves to things a bit more. They might already have been privileged and noticed that it is more acceptable to help yourself to things here in America. That things are even better here— you can have four cars here instead of two as they do in Sweden. I don't mean this in a negative sense; these new emigrants have an entrepreneurial spirit that has not been encouraged very much in Sweden, at least not before. Even if you have a money-making career in Sweden, it is easier to have that here.

Also, new emigrants are people who have realized that things are difficult in Sweden now: "Let's move abroad and get what we can!" And they don't just go to America. I think they move to other countries as well to learn, to gain experience, to get ahead in life. But they still keep their houses in Sweden—they are younger than me—and they know that they will be gone for two, three, or maybe five years. They might even come over as a couple or a family. Many are go-getters, more opinionated. They don't see America as "Now I will come here and try my luck," but they take it for what it is, and they calculate—not coldly perhaps, but they calculate—and they plan what they are going to accomplish here. They buy a car here and take that back to Sweden and so on. They have a plan—much more than what I had. I did not have a plan beyond staying in America for three years before I would return home to Sweden to work.

I read Swedish every day, and I prefer to read Swedish rather than English in the evenings because I am so tired then. Sometimes I even choose to read English books in Swedish; I buy them as paperbacks in Sweden. I probably buy 20 – 30 books a year when I go home; it's a plan. I tried to bring a book box to the coffee gatherings, but most people there only wanted to read magazines. If one organized it, and if a few other people got involved, one might be able to get a book club going. It is important to read. I feel that I can keep up with things, even the crime novels by Henning Mankell. I enjoy reading crime novels; I like the problems they present. I may not like the violence and the criminality, but I feel that you can experience the way Sweden is today in some of those books, and see how things work in general. They provide a better picture of how society works than if you read a book that just depicts a single family in the province of Jämtland, as does Kerstin Ekman's novel, *Blackwater,* for example.

I subscribe to one trade journal, *Sjukgymnasten* [*The Physical Therapist*], which I think is really good. It presents many new findings. There is progress in Sweden! Sometimes I even go back to Sweden for continuing education and deduct the expenses on my taxes with a clear conscience since I make use of what I learn in my work. And I read *Månads-Journalen* [*The Monthly Journal*] from cover to cover. I think it is really important, because it is primarily about culture and literature. It gives you a cultural kick. You feel part of the larger world again, because you are sort of on the margin here. People do not stay as informed to the same degree here.

Living here, I sometimes feel ashamed that people don't know more about the world, compared to when I lived in Sweden. The rest of the world was much more visible there, with news reporting and all that. Here it is a bit more easy-going and people don't worry as much about Bosnia, for example. People are not affected in the same way as they are in Sweden. I could certainly read more on my computer, but I don't enjoy reading newspapers online. Sometimes, when somebody returns from Sweden and brings these celebrity magazines, I realize that I have been gone along time. The celebrities are all different; they have been completely replaced during the ten or twelve years I have been here.

Because my life is so busy, I don't find the time to write letters to my friends in Sweden. I would like to do that. Some people I call. That's easier. I call my mother and father every week, and sometimes a friend. That's a tradition I have on Saturday or Sunday morning—as I put breakfast on the table, I take care of all my phone calls. I feel that my mother is up-to-date on everything that happens here. There may not be any shocking news or anything, but we keep in touch.

Once or twice a year I go back to Sweden. I suppose there have been years when I have not returned home, but then I have gone back twice the following year. I have done this since I came to the United States, but it has become more difficult now that I have a steady job. I only get two weeks of vacation. On the other hand I have liberal boss, so if I would have to take a leave of absence, I think it would be possible. But I would not be able to take six weeks off, which I really would like to do. At the same time it feels good not to have this depression-like homesickness any more, and not the sorrow over the fact that I won't be moving back. I have my Swedish identity here. I have much more security in myself than I have in some Swedish food dish or anything else. And because we have a Swedish *au pair* we have an additional connection. Now, when people ask me things about Sweden, I have started to say: "I don't know. After all, it is twelve years since I lived there, and I don't think I can answer it, because I actually don't know." I try to read the newspapers and I go back, but it is not the same as when you live in it.

I think that the Swedes of today are more like Americans, more than they were before. When I go back to Sweden, it is something of "Little America" there. When I read Swedish dailies, there are a lot of English influences—advertising and things like that. It is still difficult for me to watch Swedish advertising on television. I find it corny beyond belief. Here it is completely taken for granted, a part of the culture, but when it gets inserted into Swedish culture, it does not add up at all. I suppose that Sweden has become Americanized with commercial things and soaps on television. Perhaps Swedes eat more fast food now, and they still think that eating at McDonald's on Fridays is still something of a family party. A lot of people do it. Our family does not have any McDonald's culture at all; we hardly ever go there even though we only live a block away.

I would never have had it as good in Sweden as I have it here, even though I think I had it good in Sweden. I don't mean just financially. If I had practiced as a physical therapist in Sweden, I might have gained different experiences and qualities. Here, I have developed in a different direction. It has been a great advantage to be a Swedish physical therapist here, with ergonomics in my background. It has given me a good job. I am one of the first company physical therapists in Portland. There are not that many companies that have one. In Sweden physical therapists are being laid off now; things have changed there. That there would be unemployed physical therapists was unimaginable when I moved. I think it has been good for me to move away from Sweden. I will always maintain that I have been incredibly lucky to have grown up there. I received the best of both worlds. I got to grow up there, then come here to harvest the fruits. And at the same time you can feel that that you have the possibility to go back if you want. Or move somewhere else. What a privilege that is!

VII

I ONLY BROUGHT ONE THING WITH ME, AND THAT WAS MONEY

Tobbe (b. 1959)

Beavercreek, Oregon, 2000

The first time I came to the United States was on a golfing event, a summer exchange, in the early 1970s. An American kid came to Malmö to play golf, and the next year I got to go to the United States. This kid couldn't say "*Torbjörn*," so he called me "Tobbe," and that has been my name ever since. We spoke English to each other, but when you are twelve years old that is not very easy. He longed for home just as much as I did when I went to Cincinnati the following year. When you are that young, it is difficult to have an impression of a place, but it was fun to play golf, fun to be there. My father had the idea that I should return to the same family when I was sixteen. Everything was just great. I was there for five weeks and we had so much fun. I am still in touch with him and I am going to go visit him again this summer.

After coming back to Sweden, I signed up as a Rotary exchange student and that is how I came to the Pacific Northwest. My first six months in 1976 I spent with a family who temporarily lived in Omak, a small backwater of a place in northern central Washington. In school, we called it "the armpit of the world." Omak might have had one thousand inhabitants. It was a very bad place to end up as an exchange student, because it was so far from everything. It was narrow-minded, very narrow-minded because people were religious—something like that. There was not a whole lot to talk about. My host family in Omak was only living there temporarily to manage a paper mill. They were from Portland and have since moved back. They became my connection to Portland. It was a really nice family and we still see each other, twenty-five years later. They had two children my age, both of them a couple of years younger.

I simply could not understand that you could not buy beer until you turned 21. In Sweden they sold 3.5 beers at this time and there was no real age limit. The first time I bought beer in Sweden I was eleven years old, and I had used my weekly allowance. But I ran home and asked my mother to give me my money back in exchange for the beer so that I could buy candy instead. Beer did not taste very good. You would never have been able to do that here. I remember that I asked a guy in school if there was a discotheque where you could go and have a beer and hang out with your friends, and he answered:

"You can't drink beer; discotheques don't serve that here."

"But is there a bar where you can drink a beer?"

"No, you can't drink beer in a bar."

"Alright. Is there a saloon where you can drink a beer?"

I did not understand that it was *the beer* you couldn't drink! As it turned out, it wasn't really a problem, because in Omak we lived near the Indian Reservation, and I had an Indian friend ....

Omak was so confined and negative that I asked to be transferred to Cincinnati. It had nothing to do with the family—they were totally fine—but it was the small town mentality. Just take something like an Omak high school dance. I walked up to a girl and asked if we could dance together. Her brother, who I knew well, suddenly appeared and sternly asked me to leave her alone. I had not gone to her parents the day before and asked their permission to dance with her. For a teenager from Sweden, and from a city like Malmö, this was completely incredible. But many things were like that.

So I came to Cincinnati again and thought that it was a really fun city. It might have been slightly larger than Portland, but Portland has more growth now, so they might be about the same. With rivers running through them—Ohio River in Cincinnati and Willamette River in Portland—the cities are actually fairly similar. The difference is that the Midwest is flat as a pancake and has a difficult climate. It is muggy. When they say that the weather is "in the 90s," they mean 90 percent humidity and approximately 90° Fahrenheit. It is pretty intense. I stayed with a minister's family in Cincinnati. He was an Episcopalian, but he never said anything about me attending his church. I did go occasionally, but not regularly, and he had no objections to that.

There was no problem getting transferred from Omak to Cincinnati, but later on something came out of it. The small-town mentality took over. A man in Omak, a Rotary member who had an exchange student himself, got angry when he saw that I did not like his little town. So he turned to the INS, Immigration and Naturalization Services. The issue was that my one-year visa was only valid for the school in Omak, and you could not switch schools unless you returned to your country of origin first. It was one of those technicalities. So he informed the INS, and they came and knocked on the door in Cincinnati. This was easy for them to do because we had done everything aboveboard. They were actually very nice and said that this is insane, but we have to do this. It all ended with them saying that if I flew home voluntarily within one week of graduation—which is what I was going to do anyway—they would not keep a file on this. So everything resolved itself. Later, Rotary found out that one of their members actively had tried to make life hard for one of the exchange students. He is actually the only one I know who has been kicked out of Rotary, because they thought his behavior was totally insane.

I really fit the role of a high school senior, fell into it very quickly. In Sweden I had not been one to spend more time in school than I had to, but in the United States it was such a blast that I did not want to miss a single day. It was a completely different atmosphere with a lot of fun things to do. I can't say that I studied serious subjects like math, physics and chemistry very hard, I really didn't. But they offered fun things like photography and sports. I played golf and joined the school tennis team. I spent a lot of time with the other students. I actually had lots of fun in Cincinnati. It was incredible. It was sort of like the Hollywood movies you see about high school—boys and girls who drive cars, throw parties, and have a lot of fun. That was the life I lived, totally. Almost a little bit crazy, but fun. I got completely turned on to American radio scene, to all the music they played. Disco was hot then, and I suppose I still listen to that. We had "P3" in Sweden, and they just talked all day. American radio is still incredible; you can drive and listen to a good radio station if you don't have your own cassette tapes. So radio was a big thing for me. And television was so different. Ads were fun for me, because I had never seen them before. Advertising on TV in Sweden was prohibited! I thought it was great. My friends thought that I was a bit strange—a Swede walking around humming all the tunes from the TV ads. One thing that I thought was just fantastic: they showed a James Bond movie on TV. I simply could not understand that. They would never have done that in Sweden during the 1970s. There was a huge difference at that time.

In those days getting a driver's license was no problem. I got my driver's license in Cincinnati and had my own car. Today you are not allowed to do that as an exchange student, but then it was OK. I wanted to work in an amusement park just north of Cincinnati—it was called King's Island—but in order to do that you had to have a social security card. I just went in and got one. You can't do that any longer either; now you need a work visa first.

Platform shoes were in fashion then—I remember that. When I came to the United States we wore tight jeans in Sweden, and I suppose that looked a bit strange here. Here people wore these platform shoes and a striped T-shirt with a white collar. It almost looked like a uniform. So I got myself a new wardrobe, but not just for that reason. After all the hamburgers, I put on a lot of pounds. When I went to high school, McDonalds was *the* place; it was a big thing for me. I returned to Sweden in a light blue pinstriped suit, platform shoes, gold chains, and a big hat with a feather in it—and 100 lbs heavier. At the airport, my parents stood there looking for me without recognizing me. In Cincinnati at that time, the music was heavily influenced by black culture, and the clothes fashion followed that too. I almost looked like a pimp when I returned to Sweden.

I attended a technical high school for two years in the city of Trelleborg. We had a lot of fun there too, because we were three guys who had been in the United States at the same time, and coming back, we went through school together. I would say that we almost turned that school upside down! Cars, girls, beer, and parties every Friday and Saturday. Always. A lot of fun. After high school I did my military service, something you had to do. I actually flew back to the United States once before I went into the military. I flew both to Cincinnati and to my first family in Portland. During my entire year as an exchange student, I was dead certain that I would return to the United States. I thought of going to a university here. I looked into a number of ways to find a way to come back. But then I ended up studying economics at the University of Lund after my military service. Just after graduating, my father and I bought a real estate business in Höllviken, just south of Malmö. So I started working as a real estate agent directly after the university.

I was completely focused on going to the United States, and realized that I needed money to do it. That was the big thing—money. I bought a book about emigration. In those days you could invest $40,000 in a new business here, and if you worked with that business for three years, you were granted a temporary visa for the duration. After that, if you could prove that you could support yourself on the business you had created, you were granted a permanent visa. I don't remember now what this kind of visa was called. Anyway, I was totally focused on this and worked to raise the required amount of money. At that time I saw this as the only way to get into the United States.

I brought a small business with me over here—it sounds incredible what I actually did to get over here. It involved plants that were treated with a patented liquid. A nutrient solution made the plant open all its pores, and it was followed by a poison that brought all its processes to a complete standstill. You froze it, so to speak. Then you cut the roots off and put it in a pot with cement, not soil. It retained the same feel and look of a living plant, but never grew again. Five years later it still looked the same. It was an interesting thing, really. It was the best business I could find to do for those three years. It was a Swedish invention, and it is called Flora Dream.

I had planned to start this business in Cincinnati. By then the family I knew there had moved to South Carolina, so I commuted there a lot. Then the son in the exchange family in Omak, "my younger brother," was about to get married in Portland and they asked me if I wanted to come to the wedding. I did. That was in 1985, the driest year ever in the Portland area. So I thought—this kind of weather is good for my business. The paper mill that my exchange father had worked for had begun closing down, and he had made some money when they parted ways. He heard about my plans with Flora Dreams and got pretty interested: "Why don't we do this together here? We have a hell of a lot of plants here!"

So I moved from Cincinnati to Portland, and that

was when I took the next big step and came to the United States. We had to rent a place, buy all the equipment, and get started, so that took a while. I travelled back and forth to set everything up, and it was not until 1986 that the factory was ready. It was difficult to get the business going, but it probably would have been the same anywhere. People here like living plants just because they are alive. But I had to keep it going and after a while things picked up. I employed a girl who was a born salesman; she was simply fantastic. At this point I started thinking about expanding into the Midwest. I went to North Carolina a couple of times—it was my connection to the family from Cincinnati—and met a girl there and everything started to get complicated. I had to make up my mind: *Was I really going to move to North Carolina?* On my way out to the Portland airport I turned around and went back into town again. I called the girl who sold flowers for me here. I have never missed a plane in my life, except this time. We went out—we had just been very good friends—and somehow I stayed here and married her.

It was disadvantageous for me to get married that year—1987. I should have waited until 1988 for the sake of my visa. It was one of those technicalities again—visas are such a hassle. Early in 1987 I asked her if she wanted to get married in the fall, and in the summer we went to Sweden. Naturally, my parents wanted to meet her. When we returned to Seattle, the custom's officer looked at my passport, then at my wife-to-be, and said: "You have a visa for non-immigrants. You are only allowed to work here as an *investor*. Because you come back with an American girl, I don't believe that you are just friends." I don't remember exactly how he put it, but his point was that I sailed under false colors. When you intend to get married, you need an immigrant visa, not an investor visa. So he told me: "Either you can go to a judge and see if you can get this sorted out, or you can go back to Sweden and we will forget this happened."

I had been through this once before, so I left her there and went back to Sweden. It was easier to get all the paperwork done over there. I invited her to Sweden and we got married in the church in Skanör. After that I went over to the American embassy in Copenhagen and showed them my marriage certificate, and they put a new visa in my passport right away. Then we flew over to the States. And can you believe it: when I arrived at immigration, I got scolded again! First I thought—no, not one more time. Then he started laughing and said: "Now that you are married to an American citizen, I want you to go through US immigration even if you carry a Swedish passport." So he was only joking with me.

A new two-year period started for me then, because there are people who only get married so they can stay— marriages of convenience—something I was totally against. I would never have been able to do that, and that was the reason I got an investor's visa. Actually I had no intention to marry either—it was just something that happened. What I got was a temporary permanent visa. Typical bureaucracy! So I had to start all over because we got married a year too soon. We should never have gone abroad. But we had not understood that you can't get into the United States that way. We would have had to fly in different airplanes in order not to come together.

When I moved to the United States, I came with a suitcase of clothes, and the next time I came with my golf bag. I was sort of ready for this: I wanted to start anew for real, start over from the very beginning, buy furniture, things like that. Those were things I never really thought about. I had lived a bachelor's life in Sweden, and that's how it continued until this girl came into the picture. When I came here, I always drove a Corvette, a '69 Corvette, 400 horsepower or whatever it was. A boy's dream! I drove three or four of them, but when you turn forty, I suppose you have to quit doing that kind of thing. My old friends found out that I liked cars, and I think I sent about a dozen of them to Sweden. Now I drive a four-door Cadillac, a real estate agent car.

I still had quite a lot to do with our real estate business in Sweden. We had purchased a fairly large piece of land and built a building with 24 apartments. It started to take off, so I began to make money in Sweden, receiving checks all the time. The exchange rate with the Swedish *krona* was still pretty good, so I did not have to work. I did pretty well for a couple of years, and I began to think that Flora Dream was a bit unnecessary. Even if it did fairly well, it did not generate any real money. So I gave up my Flora Dream business. Between 1987 and 1989 I lived off of that property, and lived pretty well.

Then I felt that it was time to cut the umbilical cord and do everything in the United States. I had a permanent visa, what they call a green card, but I thought it was difficult at times. So I became an American citizen. As a real estate agent in the United States there are certain things that can be a bit irritating if you are not an American. So I sold the Swedish properties in the summer of 1989. That 24 apartment building alone sold for an embarrassingly large amount. It was almost enough to make you feel ashamed.

Two months before the crash. Totally incredible. Things turned out so badly that ten years later it sold for less than what I had been paid. The funny thing was that you are normally not allowed to take money out of Sweden, but the European Union had begun a little bit by then. They had agreed to remove this Swedish law—you know how bureaucracies are—without being able to agree on a new law. Just as I sold my properties, there were a couple of months without a law. During that time you were allowed to take money out, completely, just as you wanted. The exchange rate was six *kronor* to a dollar, compared to nine today. So everything happened perfectly.

When I arrived here on the fourth of July 1989 with all my money, it was the beginning of a new life for me. A completely new life. I only brought one thing with me, and that was money. The entire United States opened up to me. I did not start working as a real estate agent right away—I thought that I would party for a year first. Now I never had to work again in my life, because you could earn ten or eleven percent on a bank account here, and that was more than enough for me.

I started another boyhood dream—flying. I had flown a little bit with friends, but now I was ready to get my certificate. So I got a certificate and started to lease airplanes. But there was one disadvantage with this: You could not smoke in the airplanes—and I was still a smoker then—and I thought that I would buy my own airplane so that I could smoke. So I bought an airplane and got to know the man who leased airplanes at the airport. He asked me if I wanted to buy another airplane that he could lease. So I started buying airplanes in an arrangement called "lease back." The person leasing the airplane from me is then able to lease them through the flying school. It was a great business and was a lot of fun. Doing things with airplanes was a dream: profitable, fun, fantastic. But when that fellow sold his business in 1994, I sold all the planes except my own. There are about one hundred airports in Oregon where you can land. There are not even one hundred airports in all of Sweden. There are maybe five in the province of Skåne, and when you touch down, there are no restaurants or stores or rental cars if you want to go somewhere. Here, if you intend to drive to Seattle, it takes three and a half hours as long as the traffic is good. It takes 45 minutes to fly up to the airport next to Boeing. We sometimes fly up and go to Pike Street Market in Seattle. There you can find the kind of shrimp that Swedes are used to, and they package them in ice. Then we take a taxi back to the plane before we fly back home, open a bottle of wine, and eat shrimp. I remember that my father asked me if the price per pound wasn't pretty high for those shrimp. But if you have a craving for something, you have to have it, because those shrimp taste just like they do at home.

This has actually turned into a big thing for me—trying to find food that I recognize from Sweden. I have almost become an expert at this. It started a couple of years ago, when I started getting these cravings. My neighbor took me along to Estacada where we caught crayfish. I had never done this in Sweden. Then I had to call my mother and ask her how to cook them. I have to admit that I go far out of my way to eat something Swedish.

The man I bought my first airplane from owned a real estate business, and he was very impressed that a fellow my age could pay cash for an airplane. He asked what I did and I told him that that I had been in real estate in Sweden.

He asked me if I did not want to be a real estate agent with him. I said no, no, no. At that point I was not ready for it. Then he asked me if I wanted to start building with him instead. I had done that in Sweden, and he had a builder with whom he worked. I would not have to start selling houses right away, but I could build them.

So I started building with the friend of that real estate man. We built 22 single family residences during these years. Then I started thinking: *All these houses—why don't I sell them myself when I actually know how to do it?* So I started working as a real estate agent again in 1994 after having had a couple of years off flying my airplane. We still build houses occasionally, but the real estate business has grown to a size where there really isn't much time for anything else. About 40 agents work at the office. That is pretty big. As a real estate agent I sell mostly single and multi family houses. Today I have a house for sale out in west Beaverton, and one in Sandy. I sell as far south as Oregon City and Vancouver to the north. Those are the outer limits of my area. Whenever you work with something for a while, you get to know people. When you sell a house to someone who feels good about it, they will tell their friends: "If you need a real estate agent, ask Tobbe." About 90 percent of my business comes from referrals. Real estate—that is what I do. Everything else is the fun stuff I do every now and then, like buying a new airplane.

Sweden is never a simple equation. For example, take this thing that you can't show ads on Swedish television. Sweden had such boring programs! Why would you want to waste your time on things like that? In Sweden, when I came home from the real estate office at ten o'clock in the evening after having sold a house for 600,000 Swedish *kronor*, and sat down with a beer and cheese sandwich on a tray in front of the TV: "Good night from all of us at TV 1, that's all for today." Hey, I just came home from work after a twelve or thirteen hour day! I remember thinking: *You can't live like this.* You were so restrained. Radio was the same thing. If you go somewhere here, you are sort of energized by good music, while in Sweden there was some boring person who just talked and talked. Those two things, television and radio, did not suit my taste at all.

I also began to realize that if I worked really hard, it was incredibly difficult to hold on to the money in Sweden. I have always worked hard. "Work hard and play hard" as the American saying goes. But there, it was as if everyone wanted the money you had worked for. So now you could not have any fun with your money IF you could hold on to it. Another thing was this: There were no businesses that catered to the luxury aspects of life. There was no market for that in Sweden. So I think that a main thread through all of this is that I wanted to work for my money, to make money, to spend it on something completely incredible. That was a major reason I wanted to move to the United States.

In Sweden I did not fit in because I had a completely different attitude toward work. The work environment is different, very different. Work is everything to me; I am a workaholic. I will always be there if I say that I will work, six or seven days a week. That's not what people do in Sweden to the same degree. Six weeks paid vacation—what's that? It just doesn't work. In the United States you work on your vacation as well, and you don't take six straight weeks off, but you take three-day holidays like Labor Day, 4th of July, Memorial Day and so on. I don't care much about vacation—I have a good job. I took ten days once. I like Christmas Day the best, because then we go south and come back in the middle of January. When I come back, I am ready.

I spoke to my mother last Sunday, fifteen years after I moved, and she said: "Now I understand what you meant." She had recently bought a house in her own name, and suddenly, just as the price of gasoline went over ten *kronor* per liter,* had to pay property taxes for the first time in her life. It was as if something happened to her. The lights went on. Where does all that money go? What we come to is this: I had to move. I could not have made ends meet, because I was affected by the absurd taxation levels author Astrid Lindgren dubbed the "Pomperipossa effect." If I had not lived in the United States, I would have had to pay 105% in taxes. The taxes kicked me out of the country. I have been in court for six years now. In the United States you have a jury made up of equals—ordinary people in other words. But in the Swedish courts the judge and and the jury are professional jurists. I thought that I would not have any chance there. But I have won four times, and now it is the fifth time the court wants me, so I can't really say anything more about that.

My life, our life—my wife's and mine—is clearly much better than what I can imagine that it would ever be in Sweden. I have become so incredibly comfortable with it. Just look at something like the Swedish sales tax—25%—it is completely unreal. On top of that they have incorporated

---

* Due to always fluctuating exchange rates, it is difficult to give an exact conversion into dollars per gallon. At the time of writing, the price of gasoline in Sweden is approx. $7 per gallon.

it into the price so that you never see it. That is something that I had never thought about before, but now I do: They are hiding it. Here we pay 15% in what is called payroll tax; in Sweden it was 45% on your gross income. So they make a great deal of money here already. Since then, they have changed Sweden back and forth, but when I lived there, they had reached an 80% income tax. Here I never pay more than 10%. If you are Swedish, you have learned to be shrewd. I studied tax laws at the University of Lund, so I am pretty up-to-date on all that. Initially I did not pay attention to it here. I simply paid because it was so great having to pay so little. But then I started thinking about it here too, and now I have restructured my business and am really way down again.

I suppose I have given up on Sweden; I don't think you can change the Swedes. How hard do you have to slap them before they wake up? For me, it was like this: *Hello? Wake up! Good-bye!* It was exactly those words— they bring out the feelings I had when I moved. What I mean is that it will never change during my lifetime. I will sail against the wind or walk uphill the whole time. It is incomprehensible that ten or eleven percent voted for the communists in the latest election. Voluntarily. Yikes. The crash of 1989 – 1990 completely ruined my parents' life. They were hit incredibly hard because they had just invested, and that investment went up in smoke. It tore down everything they had built up before, and they retired with nothing. My mother could not handle losing all of that, and started drinking and taking pills, and the bottle and the pills just went out of control. So all of this is a bit difficult to deal with.

During the Christmas of 1989, which is the last time I

was in Sweden, I said to my wife:

"I am beginning to feel homesick. Let's go home."

"But you are home," she said.

"Not anymore," I said. She looked at me a bit strange. The reverse was now true: Oregon has become my new home. Sweden in 1989 was a gloomy time when everything started to go downhill. When I met my friends, it was not that much fun. It was as if they had remained in same place while I had taken this gigantic leap. I almost felt bad about leaving again. Somehow I think it was the turning point in some way. It took four years to feel at home in Oregon. After that I always told my parents: Come over here instead.

My father has always wanted to move to the United States. My mother is definitely Swedish. She wouldn't move in a million years. She wants "to live and die in the North," as the national anthem goes. That's just the way it is. My parents don't really understand why I moved. Until a year or so ago, every time I called, my mother asked: "So, when are you going to come to Sweden?" And then you have to repeat the same thing over and over again. It is a problem which does not have a solution. The language is a big thing for them. The longer you live here, the more you realize that it is not the words that they don't understand—it is how the words are used. For example, I met a Swedish salesman at the airport. He had been here trying to sell a new money-saving device for paper mills, and there are so many paper mills in the United States. He was really upbeat; he was so happy: "I will sell thousands of these. Every time I visited a mill, they said: 'Oh, how nice!'" He thought that it meant an order. But of course, here people only say that to be nice. The point was to be kind *and* make him leave. The Swedes don't understand that.

I did not think that I had any problems speaking English myself, but that was probably a misconception. Doing business here is, after all, different. The way certain things are phrased, makes it difficult to choose the right words. Just take a word like "*pending*:" how many Swedes understand what that means? I myself don't know what it is called in Swedish: that something will happen, but has not happened yet? That the final things are still being dealt with? That an agreement has been reached? That it is just a matter of time for the secretary to write everything out and put it in the mail? That the recipient must be given time to check the signed original contract? In fact, it means: *Nothing will change. It is just a question of the administrative routines taking their time.* When I first came here, I did not grasp this.

Nuances take time; I think I am still dealing with that. I sell fairly large tracts of land now—big contracts where a lot of money is involved—and here there are more nuances again. Lately, I have carefully tried to find a buyer for an undeveloped area. The owner has not made up his mind whether he is going to keep it or not, so he does not want to put it up for sale, but if he gets an offer, he would like to sell. Here you have to be careful with what you can or cannot say. Suddenly you have to pay attention; you can't just say, "No!" I think I was pretty direct before. If people asked me: "Would you be interested in that?" I would simply answer "No!" They would look at me a bit strange because I was so direct. Today I would have said: "That sounds really nice. Boy, that would be great! I have to ask my wife though, and I think she had something we wanted to do tonight. Other than that, it would be lovely." I have learned to conceal the facts, so to speak. The Americans really beat around the bush something dreadful. You often wonder what it was that they said—were they interested or not?

The language has been a problem between my father and my wife. No doubt about it. My father is direct, a bit of a rumbling, male chauvinist. No *"please"* or *"could I,"* just *"Give me coffee!"* To my wife! Wow! That does not go over too well. I have tried to tell my wife that it is a cultural thing, a language problem, but there is always something there in the background that makes things work less smoothly. The hardest part of having one's parents in Sweden is that you have your mother and father here for a week every year, and during that time everything is supposed to be terrific. There is no room to say: "Well, I don't agree with you." Instead you have to say: "Yes, sure, that's great." I have not been able to figure out how to make this work better. I suppose it is something one has to live with.

This afternoon I will drive over to visit my wife's grandma. She is definitely a Scandinavian, because her parents came from Gotland and Odense. We get along great with each other. She is ninety-five and still drives and gets around. It would be nice if I could have my mother close like that: "Hi mom, would you like to go out for lunch today? Play some cards, drink a cup of coffee?" say "Bye, I'll see you next week." It would have been nice if I could have that with my parents. But that is impossible; they visit for a week or ten days, something like that. I don't want them for two weeks, because I can't handle two weeks and they don't want to fly here for just one week. It is hard to tell your mother: "You can't stay here for two weeks." One more unsolvable problem. That is the flip side so to speak. Definitely. But you have to try and resolve it as best you can; it will have to limp along.

My mother called me one day—actually on my birthday—and said that she was in the hospital. Her heart had stopped. On the third try they were able to start the heart again with those electric paddles, and they had given her a fair amount of morphine for the pain. So she called me to say goodbye on the telephone. I was not ready for this. It did not make sense to go there—there was little chance that I would make it in time. Tears started flowing like water from a tap; they just came. I had never thought about this. Then this typical American thing—I had an appointment to show a house thirty minutes later—I am sitting in the car, teary-eyed, completely torn up inside, and soon I would have to open up and say: "Hi, welcome! Nice house, don't you think?" To be able to turn the situation around and still be glad—that is typically American I think. *The show must go on.* That is something we don't do in Sweden. I was a wreck for a few days—it was a critical situation—but she pulled through.

I have kept my Swedish passport, but I think it has expired now. I suppose that citizenship has always been something that is not entirely black and white. When you become an American citizen and receive an American passport, you do that in the United States. You still have your Swedish passport, because no one has taken it from you. So you still have two passports, one Swedish and one American. In the United States you are always an American, and in Sweden you can always remain Swedish because you have not told them anything else. So you are still Swedish in Sweden. If you travel to some other country, you are the citizen of the country issuing the passport you are traveling on. I don't know how it works, but I really should be able to go to the Swedish consulate here in Portland and get my

Swedish passport renewed.

When you become an American citizen, you take an oath that you renounce your allegiance to everything else, to all other countries, aristocrats, kings and potentates, and you agree "to defend the constitution against all adversaries, foreign and domestic." You have sworn an oath to do this. So from an American point of view, you are only an American. So I don't know what will happen if Sweden changes its law making it possible to be Swedish as well. Sweden can certainly do that, but it will not change the American view.

Would I consider regaining my Swedish citizenship? You should never say never, but there a couple of things I don't like that much in Sweden. As I have said previously, taxes for one thing, and I think that you have fewer rights there. You get used to the rights you have here. In Sweden they poke their nose into people's business; they don't do that here. You live freely here. Politically I am more to the right than what Swedes normally are. But only with certain things. In the United States I usually say that I am definitely a Republican when it comes to money, the economy, and everything that has to do with finance. But on social issues, when they want to censor films and books, and on the issue of abortion—which is such a major issue here—then I am completely the opposite; then I am definitely a Democrat, a Liberal. The Republicans include "the Christian Right," and that is definitely not me. They go completely against what I believe. What do guys have to do with abortion anyway? I think it is a religious issue. This is possibly a Swedish opinion, I am not sure.

Once I needed something called a *bond*, a kind of deposit or insurance from which a court of law can withdraw money if I do not fulfill my obligations. According to the company policy you had to be an American citizen to get that, and I wasn't at the time. They were shocked when I said that was discrimination. If you use a word like that in the United States, all antennae will stand straight up. If you say that someone *discriminates*, everything stops and the federal authorities come into the picture. It is a highly charged word. The man said that he did not understand what I meant. He did not see it as discrimination at all, because in his rule book it said that he could not provide this to anyone who was not an American. But it also said that you could not discriminate against minorities, Blacks, Asians, and so on. So when I questioned this, all hell broke loose. I stood my ground all the way: If you discriminate against a Swede, what's the difference from discriminating against a Black person? I did not give up, and it went all the way up to the highest boss. In the end they backed down! That was the first time I stood up to someone in the United States. There is discrimination everywhere, but I noticed then that if you are white in the United States, aged 40 to 50, life is almost too easy.

I have never regretted what I did. Everything that has happened has affirmed the fact that I moved. I did the right thing; I have never had any doubts. Not an ounce of doubt. It is almost perfect to be Swedish in the United States, so it is difficult to turn that around: Is it hard to be Swedish in the United States?

I suppose that food is a very difficult thing here for a Swede, especially the last couple of years. A simple thing that can make me skip an afternoon meeting and drive all the way out to a store in Beaverton is salt candy. Salt licorice. My mouth waters right now, just thinking about

it. I will drive there today! No one else around here likes it. Food and flavors become more important over the
years—like cheeses and cold cuts. You can't eat too many
pastries or you become a 300 pound man. I have definitely gained two pounds every year and probably weigh 30
pounds more than I did in Sweden. We still go out to eat
almost every evening, but we don't do it quite as often as
we did. We even have a stove in the house now. The first
ten years we didn't.

I am the one who makes sure that we have a Swedish
Christmas. We have a couple of dozen of those electric
candelabra for seven candles that Swedes put in the win-
dows during Christmas, one in each window. I suppose
you can call that a tradition. A lot has to do with the food
too. I stop by the girls in the German deli and tell them to
help me, because my wife only has a bunch of salads. So I
buy ham, sausages, liver pâté, pickled herring, and many
other things. And our coffee is real coffee. My wife finds
the cheeses a bit of a problem, but she likes the shrimp and
the liver pâté—and she likes *Kalles Kaviar*† on eggs. That is
the tradition I keep alive. We don't celebrate Midsummer
and things like that.

Speaking Swedish has not been a priority for me. I
married a woman from Oregon who already had two children, so being a bilingual family was not an option for
us. I would do just fine without Swedish, but things have
changed a little bit. I find that speaking it has become a lot
more fun. For example, I call my parents once a week and
I email old friends in Sweden. Sometimes I read the news-

---

† A well-known Swedish brand of smoked cod roe caviar that is sold
in a tube.

paper *Sydsvenskan* on the internet, but I really don't have time for it because of all the things I do. To find a couple of hours every week for this is hard enough. I have started thinking about subscribing to a Swedish magazine, but I have not done it yet. Sometimes I read Swedish books; the last one I read was about Vikings.

Sometimes it is very interesting to be Swedish here. People ask about how you arrived and why, about conditions in Sweden. Americans are very poorly informed. They know nothing! I suppose I don't offer a particularly positive view of Sweden when people ask. But I have tried to change that a little bit and not be too negative, because it is unnecessary somehow. There are many nice things too, and this may be the only glimpse they get of Sweden. You have to tone it down a little bit or they will get the wrong impression—nothing beyond my own subjective angry point of view. They don't get to hear about everything else, which is also very interesting.

I have not had an exchange student myself, because I have held most Swedish things at arm's length. Until a few years ago I actively kept away from everything that was Swedish: I have never looked up other Swedes but have always just mixed with Americans. I have been here fifteen years now and this is almost the first time I have spoken Swedish with anyone except my relatives. This changed just a few years ago when I wanted more contact with Swedish things. More or less, I just wanted to disappear from Sweden.

I was incredibly lucky to grow up in Sweden during the time I did. I would not want to change anything about that. If I had grown up in the United States, it would never have put me in the same circumstances that I live in now.

Everything that I have and have done is perfect for me. Getting a Swedish education, living in an ideal Sweden, having perfect parents, coming here to live, experiencing a boom instead of a bust: all that is lucky, beautiful, perfect. No matter how you look at it, I am white, six-three, and, from an American point of view, an American even if I am not. It is one of those strange things: It takes a Swede to come here to show what an American is.

VIII

I Socialize a Great Deal with Other Scandinavians

Anne (b. 1962)

Portland, Oregon, 2001

My grandmother had relatives in America that she had visited in 1952. I think my grandmother always has traveled alone, or with friends, because grandfather does not fly. She has traveled everywhere, all through Europe and twice to the United States. So in 1979 she brought me along to the United States. She had recently retired and I was sixteen. We visited the sisters of my grandmother's mother and their children. Most of them spoke no Swedish, but they thought that Sweden was very interesting. It was a lot of fun, a holiday in May. We stayed for three weeks. My grandmother's mother came from Västervik. There were nine siblings who went to America and one who stayed in Sweden—my grandmother's mother.

We went to New York first, to Long Island, where she had good friends. They were Swedes. He was a friend of hers who had moved over and become a doctor. They lived in a very elegant house. New York was an incredibly large city. Stockholm is certainly a big city, but this was a megalopolis. The number of people was just mindboggling. We also stayed in a hotel in New York City, and there you heard police sirens all through the night—they never stopped. That is something you don't hear in Sweden. My God, it's awful when you think about it! Most places in New York were nice, and we walked around a fair amount the way Swedes do. One day we ended up walking on a street on Manhattan where we should not have been. People looked at us a bit funny. A taxi driver stopped and said that we had to get in; we had come into the wrong area. We could be robbed of our purses—practically anything could happen there. Oops! So we jumped in and rode with him. I suppose we felt that it was a bit unsafe at that point.

It was very exciting to be there and all the Americans were very nice and open. For a Swede it was kind of shocking: Wow, how interested people were! My grandmother and I were standing at a bus stop when I dropped a coin. It rolled over to a man who was also waiting there and my grandmother took quite a fancy to him. He was probably ten years older than I; he was good-looking but I did not want to go out with "such an old man." In any case, he invited us to the World Trade Center. So we sat up there and I even had a drink. I was just sixteen and probably not even old enough to be let in there. Then my grandmother found out that he was a millionaire, so she wrote down his number. And I told her: "Grandmother, cut it out. I already have a boyfriend in Sweden."

Later on, thanks to grandmother, he came to see me after I had returned to Sweden. He visited us, came with a bunch of gifts, and took me out to a restaurant in Stockholm. It was almost surreal. I brought my mother along to the restaurant and explained to him that I did not know what my grandmother had told him. But I did have a boyfriend. I suppose the millionaire was rather disappointed—and grandmother too.

After visiting New York we traveled to Pasadena, in Los Angeles, to visit our relatives there. My grandmother had a driver's license but we never had to drive. Our relatives drove us everywhere. They lived in a very big house because there were five or six children about my age. That was fun. One day I visited their high school and got a very friendly reception. It was interesting for them as well—I was their "Swedish relative." Pasadena was a very happy town, upbeat somehow. In some sense it was almost like a fantasy world, because it was not at all like Sweden. We went to Disneyland and all the people who work there smile to an unbelievable degree. It is silly, really.

Then we flew up to Corvallis in Oregon to visit relatives there, staying in their gorgeous houses. All the relatives were apparently well-to-do, because they all had large houses. They had made money manufacturing aluminum ski poles. We also went out to the coast, where they had a vacation house. I thought that Oregon was great because it was more like Sweden. But I had more fun in California where I had relatives my own age and we played together, went to parties, to their school, to the beach. In Oregon I had no teenagers to be with. Before we returned home, we also went to Seattle, went up in the Space Needle and took a trip through Puget Sound.

Basically I thought that everything in the United States was great—I came away with powerful experiences and impressions. Everything was so much bigger than Sweden. It was good for my English, too. That whole trip was a lot of fun because my grandmother was a really fun person. We were close to each other. When I returned home, I was not thinking about returning to the United States. I gave it no thought at all. I traveled in Europe a little bit, visited Greece and Spain.

I started working immediately after high school. I got a job as an office temp in downtown Stockholm, which I think is a pretty good way to try out a new job because it gives you a chance to see if you like the people. We were assigned to different places and I went to a company called *ABC Tidningsservice*. It was not big, six or seven people maybe, a data processing company for different magazines and newspapers. They liked me so much that they decided to keep me. I assisted them with writing manuals, invoicing, book keeping and that sort of thing. I worked there until I went to America the second time.

I had an apartment on Lidingö. I was incredibly lucky because my grandmother had bought an apartment, and I paid the mortgage on it as rent to her. Then I met a man in a gym; he lifted weights and so did I. He lived just a few blocks away. He was an American Marine and worked at the US embassy. The Marine Corps has a large, beautiful house on Lidingö; it is owned by the embassy. There were maybe five or six bedrooms, because there were five or six Marines who worked at the embassy. They had a sauna, bar, a dance floor. They rebuilt the entire house. Those guys are party animals. Only singles lived in that house. Those who were married rented another house on Lidingö. So he invited me to the parties they had in that house. Naturally, he was incredibly charming. He came from Colorado

Springs. He wanted to go to Europe because his mother came from Germany. So he had chosen Europe and was sent to the embassy in Stockholm. When you only see five or six Marines, a small group like that, you don't really understand the nature of the entire Marine Corps.

He had been given a book about the correct way to interact with Swedes, how to treat them. His tour of duty in Sweden was only two years, and he had been there about a year when he met me. So we were together for a year. He did not speak Swedish, but he tried. He took a couple of language classes and picked up a few words here and there. But he never learned to speak it fluently, could never discuss things, so the language we shared was English, or *Swenglish*. We got married in Sweden—a big wedding at the embassy and in a Catholic church, because he was a Catholic. I am not exactly religious, and when I think about the wedding now I should maybe have raised some objections. But it is too late now.

We bought quite a lot of new furniture at IKEA before we went, and I brought a writing desk that I had. The Marine Corps moved everything. My understanding was that we were soon going to return to Sweden, because he had only two years left of his contract. That is what he said too, that when his contract was done, we would return to Sweden. It sounded like he really wanted to do that. So what I got myself committed to was not an emigration, just two years in the United States. And my family thought that as long as we came back, it was OK to move to the United States.

We arrived in Colorado Springs first and stayed there for a month; it was his vacation. It was in September and I got a driver's license there. I had lived in Stockholm where

I always used public transportation. It was much cheaper to travel by subway than to drive a car. Stockholm had excellent public transportation. But during that month I got my driver's license. I studied a small book and took the written test before I began driving. I practiced driving with my German mother-in-law. She had lived in the United States more than twenty years. She was really nice. Then I took my driver's test and wow—I had my license! It cost me $25.

The military base where my husband started working was located in Carlsbad, California, but we lived in Oceanside. It was about half an hour north of San Diego. He had no family there and we knew nobody. But he decided that we were not going to live on the base; instead we were going to rent an apartment so that it would not be too much for me. That was actually very considerate of him. When he went to work in the morning, I sauntered down to the pool, read books, and wrote letters to my friends. I also drove around and looked at things. I had a car and a map. I wanted to start working, but did not receive my green card. Apparently there was some problem with it, because it took six months. To be there for half a year without being able to work can be quite trying.

I had left Sweden, my friends, family, my job, and the only one I got to see was him. I became totally isolated. Making new friends did not happen overnight. I had a few conversations around the pool with the neighbors, but they were mostly retired people. I wanted to go back home to Sweden, but thought that I would stick it out for two years. After a while my husband got to know people through work. There was a nice American couple that we liked, as well as another couple who lived on the base. So we drove over there sometimes. The Marines had parties, played volleyball, and drank lots of beer. I also met two Swedes, but they did not like my husband, so all of us never got together socially.

There was a black family on the base that we also spent time with, and when I finally started working, it was at the same place as this black woman. It was a factory that manufactured parts for the space industry. It was a pretty monotonous job; I assembled parts. In Sweden I had worked with book keeping, so this was definitely not something I had done before. But I thought that it did not really matter what I worked with at this point. I also felt that I did not speak English fluently. I suppose I spoke it fairly well, but I could not speak good business English, and it took several years before I understood all the slang people used. Sometimes I still run across words that I don't understand.

We lived down there for a year and a half, after which my husband was supposed to work as a recruiter. So he asked me where I wanted to live. I answered that Oregon sounded pretty good. I was tired of sunshine! There was sun every day, and that is nice for a month or two, but as a Swede you are used to rain and seasons. I had been to Oregon and knew that I would like it. My husband had never been to Oregon and I had said that it was green and beautiful. When we drove up, we came through Colorado. We drove for hours through the desert and he said:

"What the hell? Is this Oregon?"

"I promise, I saw trees!" I answered.

We arrived in Portland and found out that the recruiting office where he was going to work was actually located in Milwaukie, and for some reason we moved into an apartment in Beaverton. But we quickly figured out that it was probably better if we lived in Milwaukie, so we bought a house there and moved in.

When we had lived in Portland for a total of two years, I felt that we had been in the United States long enough, and that we should move back home to Sweden. But he did not think so at all. At this point he had re-established himself in his homeland again, and moving to Sweden, by golly, that was not something he could do now. So we started arguing a little bit about this. I think I also began to get irritated about his other interest as well, which was basically limited to going up into the mountains to shoot with a machine gun. I joined him to go shooting once and that was not a great day. Brush caught on fire and fire trucks had to come up. Very embarassing. His interest in guns was too excessive. He went to gun shows all the time and bought different kinds of fire arms. I am sure he had ten different guns at home—two machine guns and eight pistols. He did not even have a gun safe. Of course, he was a Marine! Being a naive Swede—I did not get it. When you marry a Marine, well of course, guns are his job. In addition, he liked to decide things a bit too much, such as whom I could have for a friend:

"No, she has just gotten divorced. She is not a good friend for you."

"What? You think you can pick my friends?" I answered. That simply doesn't work.

When I came to Portland, I thought that I would get a job as an office temp again; it was such an easy job in Sweden. So I went to an employment agency for office temps called Kelly Girls and took a test. They provide short-term jobs at different companies that last a week or two. Pretty soon I got a job at Hannah Anderson in Portland, a business that sold Swedish children's clothes. It was owned by a Swedish woman and other Swedes worked there too. I was a good typist and I knew office work, and that was what they needed. They needed someone who could write address labels quickly, because initially they didn't have a computer. Nothing was computerized back then. I would take an order on the telephone, write it down, and type the address label on a regular old typewriter. Then I had to run and get the items that were going to be shipped. When I started working there, we were only about ten employees. For a while I worked both at Kelly Girls and for Hannah Anderson, and they asked me if I wanted to start working there full time. I hesitated, because I wanted to be able to take six weeks off in the summer so that I could go to Sweden.

"We'll give you six weeks off!" the boss said.

"OK, then I'll take it," I said.

At this point I suppose I had let go of the thought that I would move back to Sweden, because I did not know what was going on between me and my husband. I did not know what we were going to do. *OK*, I thought, *let's try a few more years and see what happens.* But in the end it just did not work out. It got to be too difficult, because he decided too much about what I could and could not do. So after four years I decided to get divorced, but it took him two years to understand that. He was a Catholic and did not want to sign any divorce papers. But when he had finally done it, he said:

"Now you're going back to Sweden!"

"What? Am I going home? You think you can decide that?"

Now I wanted to stay in Portland for a year just to

hold my own against him. In addition I had landed a good job that I liked. I liked my boss. She invited me to stay for a while at her place after the divorce, and I lived there for a month or two. It was really hard to get my own apartment. I had no credit. All the credit cards had been issued in my ex-husband's name. So it was a question of trying to get the person who rented the apartment to believe in me. That was difficult. Finally I got my own apartment in Northeast Portland and it felt good to be independent in the United States. Then I thought that I would go back home.

You are supposed to divide everything up when you get divorced, and I took some things. But my husband was very difficult to deal with. He did not think that I should have anything, because I was moving back to Sweden. The lawyer said that we actually had to share, and it was agreed that I would get the car and some of the furniture. But there was no car left when I was supposed to pick it up. He had gotten angry and driven around very fast and crashed it. It was such a rotten way to treat me! So then I had no car. I was forced to cash out my entire retirement savings in order to buy a car and furniture. I don't know what has happened to my ex-husband, but I get a Christmas card every year from his parents. It is kind of funny, because I have never written back. But maybe I should. More than ten years have passed since the divorce now. After the divorce my mother thought that I should come home, but my father thought that I would be able to take care of myself over here. When my father was really young, he had been a sailor and traveled around the world. He thought that Sweden was irritating, that the taxes were really horrible. He is negative about all the rules, about the entire system.

After living alone for just a few months, I met another man. That was unfortunate for my mother and my father. When I met him, he was working in construction. He was doing a remodel where I was working. It was a historical building on 10th Avenue. There was a storefront on the street, but other than that everything was very old—mostly a shell that had to be rebuilt on the inside. They worked their way up, floor by floor. Finally, I ended up on the fourth floor with the book keeping department. We were the only ones there; the rest were construction workers. That is how we met; he came into my office sometimes.

My plans to move back home gradually changed, and for every year that passed they diminished. I felt more at home here. I was together with my new boyfriend for a year, and then we bought a house together. We were not married then. He was born in San Francisco but both his parents were born in Portland. They had moved to California when his father had become a biology professor at a university there. So he had grown up in California, but then they moved back here when his father retired.

We went to Sweden before we got married. We were only there for three weeks, but it was a shock for him—the language barrier for one thing. And he thought that there was more action in the United States, more things to do. He also found the US cheaper. When we went to Sweden, the exchange rate was five or six *kronor* for every dollar, so everything was really expensive. And he discovered that he could not buy the beer he wanted in a regular grocery store. He thought it was very nice to visit and everything, but he did not know if he could settle in Sweden. He enjoyed his American friends. In order to stay in construction in Sweden, he would have to switch to a new language, to Swedish building codes, to meters and millimeters from feet and inches, and so on. All that would just have been too much for him. In a worst case scenario, he might have been able to do it, but when I married him, he said: "You know, honestly, I actually don't think that I can move to Sweden."

We got married in 1992 and at that point I made the decision to stay in the United States. I married him because I was really in love with him. If I really wanted to move back I might be able to talk him into it. When I got married again, I had lived in the United States for more than five years, and things felt better and better. Now I know that I will always live here, but I still don't feel like an American. I will never become an American; I will always be Swedish. I could certainly take dual citizenship and be both American and Swedish, but I am still Swedish.

My husband has his family here and that was maybe why I said it was alright to stay. I think I have a good relationship with his family. Everyone keeps in touch and there are no great family feuds. We see each other often, every time one of his brothers has a birthday, and sometimes we also get together when one of the wives has a birthday. When one of the children has a birthday, we celebrate that. Sometimes we go out to the coast together. Basically we do something every month. So there is regular contact and all of this feels important.

Sometimes my husband gets this idea that he would like to move to a place that is warmer, but I say no to that, absolutely not. I definitely want to be close to his family. Family was very important to me in Sweden too—to be close to my mother and father, all my grandparents. I would be capable of living in a warm climate as long as the family was there. We like it here and we have es-

tablished friendships, Swedish friends, and I belong to a
Scandinavian group. I will soon turn forty, so ... this will
have to do. I almost feel like I do in Sweden. Oregon's
nature is Swedish—almost. I speak Swedish more or less
every day, either with other Swedes at work, or because
I sometimes have to call Sweden for my work. I have
settled down in Oregon.

You get stuck, especially when you have children.
That is why you become more Swedish and search out
other Swedes. Now I have realized: *Oh my God—I won't
return.* I have enrolled the children in the Swedish school
and keep in touch with the Swedes who are there, and I try
to speak Swedish to the children—something which is almost impossible when you work. I work full time, but I do
it on a four day work week. My hours are the same as my
husband's—we leave together and come home at the same
time. It is difficult, because the children speak English all
day until I come home at six o'clock in the evening. Then
when you say something in Swedish, they have a temper
tantrum on the floor, cry and scream: "No, no, no, don't
say that! It's wrong!"

My husband does not speak Swedish, so English is our
language at home. When my oldest son was little, I only
read Swedish books to him. For a couple of years I managed
to convince him that it was actually impossible to read in
English. But after he had turned three, he realized that Dad
actually could read in English! So that ruined it. Things
haven't been the same since—just some homework from
the Swedish school. But that is nothing; you can't learn
Swedish from that. Trying to maintain Swedish when my
husband does not speak it is almost impossible. Before my
oldest son was born, I looked for a Swedish daycare center,

or some kind of private Swedish daycare arrangement, because I knew that I had to start working again after three months. So I was aware that the language situation would be difficult. If there had been a Swedish babysitter, things would probably have worked out, but I could not find one. There is no Swedish daycare center either, but if there was, it would be worthwhile to drive the children there.

I am active in the Swedish school. It runs for two hours on Saturday. Everything is done entirely in Swedish. About half the children speak Swedish, half English, but there is at least more Swedish than English and they get Swedish class mates. After three years I am still the school treasurer because no one else wants to do it.

When I lived down in San Diego, we had no family there. Here there is so incredibly much to do, something almost every weekend—the children's school, American friends, Swedish friends, dinners, relatives. Then there is work: homework with the children, helping my husband with his office work, the Swedish School. Life is fast-paced. In spite of that I only feel stressed at work. Thirty hours is too much. I need more time with my children. I worked forty hours before and got to see my children two hours in the evening. I could speak a little Swedish before bedtime. That is why I want to work less; I am trying to do that now.

Being Swedish in the United States has been very positive. For example, because I am white and blonde, I never get stopped on the street: "Can I see your green card?" No one has ever asked for it. When people hear that I speak English with a Swedish accent, when I tell them that I come from Sweden, they will say: "Wow! How interesting." But it is true, of course, that many Americans will say: "Sweden? Switzerland?" They don't really know the difference between various countries and there are many who don't even know where Sweden is on a map. Those Americans who know something about Sweden think that it represents high quality. They like Volvo even though it is fairly boxy and ugly. And they know that Swedish taxes are high. Taxes here make Americans upset, so the taxes in Sweden make them even more upset. But Americans are not well-informed about Sweden.

When I lived in California, people talked pretty fast, and I thought that it was hard for them to slow down and try to understand me. It is true that I had not been in the United States for very long at that time, but it was somewhat difficult. I had to explain myself several times. In general, I think that people in California discriminate more. There is less discrimination in Oregon and it is much more open to all ethnic groups. Portland is a good city. I like it here.

It is nice that Americans don't care about clothes and fashion the way people do in Sweden. You don't have to dress like everybody else. Everybody has their own style and that is fun. That is not the way it is in Stockholm. There, everyone is supposed to look the same and you have to wear the latest fashion. In the United States you can look like a clown and no one even looks at you funny. That is pretty nice. People don't give a damn about how they look. Totally.

Take something like family gatherings in America: when you eat, people sit all over the place. They stand up, they sit down—anywhere. In Sweden, everyone sits down together around a table. Swedes like to sit down around a long table and talk and discuss things. Here they spread

ANNE

out and sit any which way. That really bothers me; I have never been able to get used to that. When I have a Christmas dinner at my house, even if things are pretty tight, I put two tables together in the living room. We are a fairly large group since my husband has three brothers. I make sure that we have enough tables and chairs so that everyone can sit down together. And if someone doesn't, I tell them to. It is a Swedish Christmas table with ham, pickled herring, meat balls, small Swedish sausages, anchovy, Jansson's Temptation, crisp bread, cheese, shots of *aquavit* ....

But my big tradition is the crayfish party. It began when a couple of us thought that it would be fun to have a crayfish party in August. I said: "Why don't we go up into the mountains and try to catch some crayfish?" We did and then we had a small crayfish party. I did not know very many Swedes then because I did not have any children and the Swedish school was not yet in existence, and I did not attend the Swedish women's coffee gathering. So in the beginning the party consisted of a mix of Swedes and Americans, and it was very popular. Then we did this every year. I think my crayfish are the tastiest. There are those who compare my crayfish with those served by the Swedish Consul here in Portland—and they say that mine are much better!

We catch somewhere around 300 – 400 crayfish which I cook up at Timothy Lake the traditional Swedish way, then we chill them on ice and freeze them for a couple of weeks. We normally catch the crayfish in June and July. My husband has professional diving equipment and he dives for the really big crayfish. We have had this crayfish party for seven or eight years now. We were seventy people last year. We were not just Swedes, but Danes and Norwegians

190

too—the entire Scandinavian community. They have cray-fish traditions in Norway, and in Denmark ... well, I don't know, but they eat them and they especially like drinking shots of *aquavit*. This has become so big that I sometimes think: *Oh my god, I can't do this any more.* But everyone says: "You have to! It has become a tradition to come to your crayfish party."

I socialize a great deal with other Scandinavians. There were a couple of women who started a Scandinavian group, sort of like the Swedish women's coffee gathering, but it was Scandinavian: Swedes, Norwegians, and Danes. With the Norwegian women I might speak Swedish, but with the Danes I can't speak Swedish. I can't understand Danish. But we still feel this Scandinavian connection, even though we speak English. It is quicker for us to speak English to each other. The group is not very big, not quite twenty people, and it has met for seven years now. We don't want it to get too big, because then we can't meet at each other's homes. For example, one woman lives in an apartment and can't accommodate more than twenty peo-ple. The Swedish women's coffee group has seventy mem-bers, and then some people can't host them all. That's not fair. This group does not want that to happen. I have been part of it since it started. It might be true that I feel more Scandinavian here—that we had so much in common was definitely not something I thought about in Sweden. You feel a lot smaller here. That is why it is so important to stay in touch and remain friends. We have a lot of fun together and everyone really enjoys each other's company. Actually I think that the Swedes in Oregon seem happier than the Swedes in Sweden. They keep in touch more, talk more with each other. In Sweden people are more reserved and don't start discussing things with each other as quickly as people do here. If you meet a Swede, you will say: "Hi, how's it going? Where are you from?" In Sweden you can't do that with every Swede you meet!

I think that everyone in this Scandinavian group are better friends, are more positive, than we would have been in our native countries. I believe that we are so incredibly positive and happy because we know each other and because we are so few. It means a lot more to be friends. You stick together, you have traditions, and you have parties. My crayfish party for example—my god what fun we have! And afterwards everyone says: "Wow, what wonderful people you had at your party." Everybody drinks *aquavit* and the mood is really great; everyone is so happy. Everyone is in good spirits. They enjoy meeting so many other Scandinavians. The mood is very different from Sweden. I mean, seventy people in Sweden might end up in fisticuffs.

Americans are always so cheerful, but sometimes I find that can be false too. You never know if they really like you, or if they are just polite. You have no clue. Sometimes they actually dislike you, but will still act positive.

I don't know how to bake, but I have become really good at cooking Swedish food. That was not something that meant anything to me in Sweden; I never thought about all the Swedish things I did. When I came here and saw all this American food, I started longing for meatballs and Jansson's Temptation and pickled herring. So I began cooking Swedish food in the United States. Swedish pancakes. I make meatballs and keep lingonberries at home. I buy herring when I visit Sweden and pickle it using my father's recipe. Swedish food has become very important to me now. I never thought about it until I came here. All the fun Swedish traditions—now I encourage them. Now I appreciate everything. And we do it to excess too, with a really big crayfish party, lots of Swedes and Scandinavians, and we lead the singing and make sure that everyone sings. In Sweden they probably think that we are nerds, but we have to have this. You could say that I have almost become more Swedish here than I was when I lived in Sweden.

In many ways, the United States is a more difficult country to live in.... It is a tough country; there are so many inequities. It is called the richest country in the world, and still so many children go hungry. This is something you discover more and more the longer you live here. Some people have health insurance and some people can't get any. Those who are extremely poor may get help, but ordinary poor people get nothing. Everything depends on what kind of insurance you have. If you don't contact your physician and go straight to a hospital emergency room, it may take several months until the insurance company pays the bill. If you are out of luck, they may not pay at all, and you get punished with a bunch of bills left and right. So compared to Sweden the health insurance situation is a real hassle. If you are unlucky, you can get too sick: "Sorry, you are too sick. Unfortunately, we can no longer insure you. Thank you for all your payments over the years." This is the flip side of the American health care system. Once you turn 65, you can get Medicare—then they have to take you—but before you turn 65, anything can happen. You pay several hundred dollars every month for your insurance, and then suddenly you get nothing after paying all those years.

Sweden does not exactly have great health care either any more. So many mistakes have been made in Swedish hospitals with my mother that it is a miracle that she is still alive. I am a Democrat and I really hope that the Democrats win the next election. If the Democrats would have been in power now, I believe that American society would be a lot better.

I think they are a little bit too generous in Sweden. It really should be stricter, but not as severe as in the United States. For example, in Sweden there is an incredible amount of paid sick leave available; here, you get no money at all if you are sick. That is not right either. Here you may be forced to use up your vacation time instead, and you only have a certain number of vacation days. My vacation these days is somewhat longer than at most other jobs, partly because the company has been Swedish-owned, partly because I have worked there for so long. But with most jobs, you get a week or two the first two or three years. It is possible that you get two to three weeks after ten years. That's awful! This is where you miss Sweden with its legally mandated vacation. Sometimes in the US, it feels like you have to work until you are nearly dead. I work a lot when I am sick; I have worked sick both in December and January. The reason for working while sick does not primarily have to do with getting paid, but because there is such pressure on me to come to work. I am the only one who fully knows my job, so there is no one else to help me. That is not good, but there are many Americans who are in similar situations: other people at work don't really know what you do.

When my youngest child was born three years ago, I had a five-month long maternity leave. I went back home then. Since then I haven't traveled back to Sweden. On average I suppose I have gone back every other year. When I first came here I went back almost every year, then it was every other year, and now when I have two children there are suddenly so many expenses. I have traveled alone with the children. The whole family went once and we have considered going next summer, but it is expensive to travel in the summer.

My brother came and visited after a couple of years, and my mother has come every fourth or fifth year. My father has never been here. He claims that he can't leave his dogs. They have German shepards. Or he might be afraid of flying—but he has never said that. He has never flown.

Friends from Sweden visited me a few times during my first years here. After that visits have become more and more rare. I had about ten friends in Sweden I kept in touch with when I left. Some just disappeared—they never wrote and told me where they have moved. They were friends from junior high and high school. I only have one really good friend left. We mostly write emails to each other and I call her every now and then. She is an old friend from junior high. We started fourth grade together. That is a lot of fun. I suppose there is no simple explanation why friendships end, but perhaps it is tiring to have a friend so far away. I don't know. It is easier now with email; sitting down to write a letter is a lot of work. Some friends had children and it is difficult to find time for it all. Everything takes so much time.

When I visit Sweden, I feel like a tourist, a visiting tourist. I am there for a short visit, I know that, and I know that I won't stay there. It is fun to come back home. It was very difficult to move away from the ambience of Stockholm, because I miss the old buildings, the churches, the old streets, Stockholm's Old Town, walking on cobble stones. I suppose I thought about the historical heritage a little bit when I lived there, but living here now, I think about it a lot. When I get to Stockholm, I make sure that I visit the Old Town. On the other hand the number of people in Stockholm during the summer is simply amazing. You can hardly move around there any more.

I see no reason to move back to Sweden because I have my family and relatives here. On the other hand, I have a deep longing for my mother and father, and I wish they were here. My mother and father should really just move over here. My family in Sweden is all spread out anyway, because my parents do not live in Stockholm anymore. My grandparents live in the vicinity of Figeholm outside Oskarshamn, and my brother lives in Stockholm. My cousins also live in Stockholm. I write to them every Christmas, but they never write back. What I mean is this: here, in Oregon, I have a lot of friends, a large family, and my sons have so many cousins. What would they do? Really, there would be nothing if we moved back to Stockholm. My children would not have a single cousin there.

The changes that have happened in Sweden are mostly things that I have read about—that there is more violence, more murders, more hate. What was the last thing I read? An old person in the hospital died from mange! It is as if the system is collapsing more and more. I don't really see it, because I am never there for more than three weeks, sometimes only two. The time passes so incredibly fast you hardly have time to blink, and then you don't get the same kind of impressions. But I read about it, I hear my mother and father talk about it, and it is pretty unpleasant. I hope that they keep Sweden Swedish, just as I think that Greece should stay Greek and Spain Spanish. You have to preserve the culture the way it is, otherwise traveling would be boring. The United States is built by immigrants, and that's the way it should be. Everyone is an immigrant here: every culture is gathered here. What is important is that the Swedes in Sweden preserve their culture—not by suppressing other cultures—but by not forgetting their own. It is as if the Swedes don't realize—like we do here in the USA—that they do have a fantastic culture.

IX

WHEN I VISIT SWEDEN, I NOTICE HOW MUCH I HAVE CHANGED

Peter (b.1963)

Lake Oswego, Oregon, 2000

I don't know exactly why I decided to take a year abroad as a foreign exchange student; for some reason I always wanted to move to the United States. I grew up with films and music from the United States, so it probably had to do with checking out how things really were. I came to Gig Harbor, which is located outside Tacoma, Washington, in 1981 as a senior in high school. I did not choose the place myself; I was assigned to it. At that time I did not even know where Washington was located. When I received the first letter, I thought it was Washington, D.C. Then, after searching for a long time on a map for Gig Harbor, I realized that it was located on the West Coast. Gig Harbor was really nice when I was there, because it was still a small fishing town then. Now people have started moving away from there because it has become so crowded. When I lived there, the nearest store was in a small gas station that an old lady had run her whole life; now there are big super markets and fast food chains.

I was 17 years old when I arrived and the family was something of a culture shock. He was a sheriff and she was a housewife. They had two children, a girl who was six and a boy who was fourteen or fifteen. They were really unorganized. They lived in a small ranch style house and they had a typical old American pickup. In Sweden I was used to wooden floors and a house that was clean and nice and with a fairly high standard, but this was a new experience with things scattered all over the place. When I arrived, they did not even know where I was going to sleep. The first day I was there, they cleaned up the TV room and put in a bed. I ended up living there for a year. I had many reasons to change host family. The parents did not get along that well; there were lots of strange things going on. A couple of times it was difficult, but I managed. At least I learned a lot. I certainly got to experience another reality, share that culture, and learn a lot more than if I had stayed at home living an ordinary Swedish life. I also felt I had to show them respect, because they had agreed to take me in. Even if they were poorly organized and may not have met my requirements, they had invited me for a year and provided me with room and board.

There were many rules within the family that seemed very strange to me. In Sweden, I was used to taking a lot of responsibility for myself and could come and go pretty much as I pleased. In those days in Sweden there was not much crime, people did not disappear or get killed, so parents let their kids run around. They did not worry too much if you were out until two or three in the morning. The worst thing you could do was drink liquor. No one thought that you could be abducted, for example. In the United States people think about these things more, but you don't understand that when you are 17 or 18 years old.

At that time in Sweden there was no cable TV, so I had not seen anything beyond what was shown on either of Sweden's two available channels. Here, these slightly older American television shows made a strong impression on me, *Lucy Ball* and *Three's Company*. I was not used to sit coms, and American football or baseball was not something I had seen before. There were television programs almost twenty-four hours a day. Perhaps I watched television slightly more on Saturday and Sunday mornings, which one did not normally do in Sweden because there were no programs on the air then.

I was fairly fluent in English when I arrived, and could understand some slang because I had seen a lot of movies and listened to music. Certain things were problematic— when there were words I did not know, and when I translated Swedish idioms into English so that no one understood what I meant. Of course, I didn't realize that what I had said was wrong, so I suppose I sounded a bit strange sometimes. But my spoken English worked pretty well and I did not experience major problems.

School was very easy. I had attended a technical high school in Sweden for two or three years, so when I studied physics in Gig Harbor, the teacher had to bring his second year college text books so that I would have something to do. What they did in high school, I had done several years ago. I could get an A without any effort—a good thing, because it gave me time for other things. I did not have to worry about academics. I had one B and A's in everything else, and I did not study very hard. I did some sports, played basketball. It was easy to make friends, and there were different groups just like in Sweden. There were *jocks* that were into sports, *nerds* that studied harder, *outsiders* and *oilers*. It was interesting to discover the dynamics among all these different groups. It was very different from Sweden, where the student body was more homogenous.

Gig Harbor was a small place. The high school was brand new and had a couple of hundred students. Everybody knew everybody. I was the only Swede but there was a girl from Finland there too. Everyone immediately knew who I was, but I did not know anybody. I wore red Converse basketball shoes; this was not anything special to me. I had worn shoes like those for a long time, but the American students had never seen them. I also wore chessboard-checkered pants because I was interested in *ska* music,* and they had never seen that in Gig Harbor either. I think they thought I was somewhat strange. I suppose that was both positive and negative, but mostly positive. I met my wife there, or she met me, depending on how you look at it. She thought I was from Australia. Later she unfortunately discovered that I came from Sweden, but I suppose it was already too late. It turned out that she lived next door— there was only a small grove of trees between us—so I could walk over to her house. She had her driver's license and a car, which gave me a great deal of freedom.

According to the rules of the exchange program, I was not allowed to get a driver's license during my stay in the United States, but the father of my host family thought

---

* *Ska* music originated in Jamaica in the late 1950s and was the precursor to reggae.

that I should have one. So I did get a driver's license, but hardly drove at all. It was fairly complicated to have to rely on others so much: if I wanted to go somewhere in the evening or on a weekend, a host parent or a friend had to drive me. In Sweden you could get around on your own—ride a bicycle, take the bus, or walk. In Gig Harbor I lived in a rural area and took the bus to school. It was too far to walk or bike if I wanted to go somewhere. I was isolated.

We took a couple of trips. We drove to Idaho once and rafted on a river, and for Christmas we drove from Washington down to Arizona. We went through the desert, through Utah, did some sightseeing and saw Hoover Dam. Coming from Sweden and arriving in Arizona for the first time was a tremendous experience. It was Christmas time, almost 90 degrees out, and cacti growing everywhere!

It was hard to keep in touch with Sweden, because in those days it was very expensive to call. I think the first minute cost three or five dollars, and every minute after that a couple of dollars. I called home once a month and I tried to make these calls very short. The internet did not exist, and there was no email, so you had to write letters.

It was fun to be in Gig Harbor for a year even if there were problems with the host family. It gave me an understanding of another culture, of different people, and I learned to take care of myself. I lived with people I didn't know, and I had to try to figure out how things worked. As a visitor to another culture, I had to learn to respect it. I am no longer in touch with the host family. They got divorced after I went back to Sweden, and for many years I chose not to keep in touch. My experience of them as people was not that positive. I went up to Gig Harbor once and saw the mother, and when my son was born she came down to visit. She gave us her address in Gig Harbor, but since my father-in-law has since moved from there, we have not bothered to go there. The last time I saw the mother was when she invited my wife and me for lunch. We thought it was a friendly social visit, but after fifteen minutes it turned out that she only wanted to sell Amway products. The last thing I heard about the father was that he had moved to South America after having been fired for criminal activities.

After my year in the United States, I think I knew that I would move back. It was fairly clear to me. I don't know if I had analyzed it very much, and I suppose that I did not really know how it would happen. I knew that I wanted to move back home for the time being, finish my studies, do my military service, and work for a while to make some money. I don't know if you can call it *a love of adventure*; maybe it was the possibilities, something different. Perhaps it could have been England or Australia. I remember that I definitely thought about moving to England. I don't know if it was fluency in English that mattered. I suppose that the United States seemed more exciting.

I moved back to Sweden in June when the school year ended, then I came back to the US for a week around Christmas to see my girlfriend. She moved to Sweden the following summer. Initially she came for three months to check things out, then she moved back to the United States for a while to work and earn some money before she actually decided to move. It was a huge experience for her; she was only eighteen and had never been abroad. Her first experience at the Landvetter airport was horrible. The passport officials took her to a private room and grilled her for fifteen minutes. After that, the customs people even looked through her wallet and the shoes she wore.

After taking that class called "Swedish for Immigrants" she started at the University of Gothenburg, where she studied English and learned that there was a difference between British English and American English. The teachers were old Englishmen who thought that the Queen's English was the only proper form of English. That was also a cultural shock for her. She did not get a residency permit and work visa the first time she applied. The Swedish immigration and naturalization services thought that we were too young! But we were persistent and she finally got her visas. We had to go to the police every six months for an interview, and we were interviewed separately to ascertain that we really lived together. Once she had received her residency permit and work visa, she worked for a while assisting elderly people in their homes. Later she worked as a translator.

When we had lived in Gothenburg for a year, I was drafted, and unfortunately I did not get to stay in Gothenburg so that I could go home every night. For some reason I was assigned to a commando unit in a town called Karlsborg. Before I left, I had told her that I would call her when I arrived there. But it was go, go, go as soon as we got there. It was impossible to call home, because I was suddenly sent out on a field maneuver for several weeks. There were no public telephones there. So she had no idea what was going on and ended up alone in an apartment in Gothenburg. That was difficult. She spoke Swedish fairly well—she had lived there for a year—but did not have very many friends. So she became pretty isolated. I got out of that commando unit after a while because I was a vegetarian and there was no food for me. Instead I ended up in the city of Borås. Things were a bit more normal there and I could usually go home on the weekends. I was supposed to have stayed in the Army for fifteen months but managed to get out after twelve. It was during this time that we got married. It is hard to believe this now that we are older, but we actually married because it was the only way for me to get a leave for a couple of weeks. We would have gotten married anyway, but my military service definitely accelerated the marriage.

Initially it was difficult for my wife because she did not know anything about Sweden beyond what she had read. It was very difficult to get to know people, feel that she really knew somebody. She had lived in Gig Harbor for a long time, and her best friend—whom she had known for a long, long time—still lived there. In the United States it is easy to get to know people superficially, but when you come to Sweden, I think it easy to get the impression that Swedes are reserved and almost unpleasant because no one says "Hi," no one smiles, no one speaks loudly. People stick to themselves. But then she made some friends and things got a little bit better. At that point she had lived there, learned the language, and started to get the hang of how things worked. It turned out that there were quite a few Americans living in Gothenburg, and she met some that she got to know. Towards the end I think things were going pretty well for her.

She had bad luck too, because the four or five years that we lived there were the coldest winters in Gothenburg's recent history. It snowed, tons of snow every year. Gothenburg is a bit unique in that the winters are damp and windy. When rainy and stormy weather is followed by below freezing temperatures so that the harbor freezes over, then Gothenburg is frigid. After we had moved away from there, the city did not get snow for I don't know how many years.

We had decided that we were going to live in Sweden for four or five years, and then were going to live in the US for ten years. We had considered Australia a possible alternative, but the biggest problem was that we did not have any connection to it. In addition, it is located on the other side of the earth. So from a practical point of view, it was not as attractive. I found many aspects of Swedish society very difficult to deal with—bureaucracy, career opportunities, and taxes. In this regard the United States seemed more tempting. In Sweden I was often frustrated with people who did not care about their jobs, with poor service, and with things that never seemed to get done. People did not want to work hard because of the taxes. They were not motivated, because work did not pay. If you had a job somewhere, you could not get fired. This was very obvious when I worked for the company Ericsson. Many people there just pretended to work because they knew that they could not be fired.

I had worked for Ericsson for a couple years and I guess I had become somewhat tired of it, and my wife was pretty homesick. So we made a decision: *OK, let's move.* That was in 1987. As I mentioned, we had gotten married when we lived in Sweden. In order to obtain a work and residency visa in Sweden you don't have to be married; you just have to be able to prove that you have been together a while. But in the United States a marriage certificate is the only thing that counts. Applying for a visa was complicated. I was supposed to have a letter from the FBI proving that I was not a criminal. I had to have a medical exam. I had to fill out forms and travel to the US embassy in Stockholm for an interview. Finally, because we did not have very much money, we had to get a sponsor in the United States who would guarantee that he would pay for my ticket back to Sweden if I ran out money. It was my wife's grandfather who sponsored me.

We sold all our furniture, and what we could not bring, we left with my mother or father. Everything else we packed up in small boxes and sent. It was mostly books. In those days it was cheap to send packages by boat, so I filled box after box with things and took them to the post office. The boxes arrived three or four months later. It worked really well.

We came to my father-in-law in Gig Harbor first, and then we stayed with my mother-in-law in Tacoma for a while. Initially I thought that getting a job would be easy. When I had applied for a job in Sweden, I just applied to a couple of employers and got a job almost immediately. There were many jobs in engineering in Sweden then. So I did not worry much about it when we came here. We took it easy and went on a vacation. After a couple of months it became a bit more urgent that I find work. I learned how you apply for a job in the United States and what a résumé was—I did not have a clue! When I got my first phone interview, I began to realize that this might be more difficult than I had imagined. First they asked if I was from Switzerland. Many Americans can't keep "Switzerland" and "Sweden" apart. Then they started asking, "Ericsson? What is that?" In Sweden everyone knows what Ericsson is, but in the United States at that time, and especially on the West Coast, no one had heard about that company.

At that time, almost all companies in engineering in

Seattle were focused on PCs and Microsoft. I had no direct experience with—or any real desire—to start working with software for PCs, and I realized that there were very few companies in Seattle that did the things I had done at Ericsson. Almost the only alternative left for me was Boeing and I did not want to work there. So I started applying in different states. When we had been in the United States for six months, I had $1,500 left and still no job. We had saved up $10,000 in start-up capital, and $1,500 was just a little bit more than what an airline ticket home would cost. What should I do: *Buy a ticket and go back to Sweden? Take the chance and stay for a few more months?* If we did, I had to find work. So I made a decision: *I'll take a chance and stay and see what happens.*

So I took a job as a computer salesman, but it did not go well. I did not even have a basic salary; the only thing they paid for was gasoline. My entire income was based on commissions. First of all I had no experience as a salesman, and secondly it was a small company. Basically my job consisted of going out and finding customers. Furthermore, it would take—which I did not realize at the time, and that was perhaps naïve of me—several months before I would even find a customer who would buy something. I never sold anything, so I never made any money. In retrospect it is hard to understand why I took a job like that, but I knew that I had to do something, I just could not sit at home and wait for something to happen.

I got called to Boise, Idaho, for my first interview. The company had sent me a ticket. On the morning of my departure I had only figured on an hour's driving time to the airport, but because of the rush hour traffic I missed my plane. I got a seat on the next plane, but it was not completely unexpected that I did not get that job. A week or so later a head hunter called me and said that a company he represented might have a job that matched my background. It turned out to be a small company in Portland that constructed telecommunication devices—telephones and answering machines. We had been to Portland once and thought that it was a nice city. The head hunter interviewed me in Tacoma. During the interview, in the middle of a sentence, he fell asleep. I just sat there wondering if this was real. He woke up about ten minutes later and continued the sentence without missing a single word. We both acted as if it never happened. Now I realize that he suffered from narcolepsy. In spite of that, I got the job the last week before I was completely out of money. They offered me a fantastic salary—I think it was $29,000 a year. When I worked for Ericsson I had been paid approximately $1,000 a month, and that was after having received a raise, so this was a completely incredible salary that I had not even dared to dream about. I was used to the way it was in Sweden—a good job that was poorly paid. So in the end I got a job after all, and the company moved us down to Portland. That was in the beginning of 1988 and we have lived here ever since.

At Ericsson, and this is true for Sweden in general, when they employ somebody, they employ a person. In the US, they employ experience. The Americans want a very specific experience, and that difference was a cultural shock to me. It was something that was different and hard for me to understand. Swedish companies have, as part of their culture, greater long-term planning, but I also think hiring has to do with workplace laws. When a company employs somebody in Sweden, they can't just fire them later, so people can do almost anything. In the United States, especially in Oregon, if they employ somebody who does not work out, they can fire them with no reason and hire someone else. In the US there is more emphasis on specific experience. It is not, as many Swedes might think, that US companies fire people left and right and for no good reason. Companies don't, but if something goes wrong, it can be fixed.

It took some getting used to the winters in Portland. Even if Sweden can get a fair amount of rain, I was not used to the constant clouds and rain we get here during the winter months. There have been many times when I wanted to move away from here and go someplace sunnier. In the United States you can basically choose any climate you want—tropical climate, snowy winters, or something in between. We have been close to moving to Arizona a couple of times, but my wife does not like heat. Oregon has an in-between kind of climate—the winters are never too cold and the summers never too hot. It would be hard for me to move further north. I actually find this a pretty pleasant climate. In the end, when you consider everything, Oregon is a pretty nice place.

We have no extended family in Portland; my wife's sisters live up in Seattle, her father in Olympia, Washington, and her mother down in San Diego. Now that we have small children, we have realized how significant a family can be, so it is not family ties that keep us here. If I wanted to, I could move down to Silicon Valley in California any time and get a really good job with an incredible salary. But I have no desire to sit in traffic, deal with the problems they have down there, and pay three or four times as much for a house. I don't want to be to be locked in like that. Oregon has many different climates and you can do almost anything: drive up to Mt. Hood if you want to go skiing, or drive out to the coast in an hour and a half.

My whole family is still in Sweden; I am the only one who moved abroad. On my father's side—several of grandfather's cousins—immigrated to America during the Great Migration, but I don't know much about them. I don't have any particular histories or contact. My family in Sweden might have had opinions about my emigration, but they never said anything. My mother never tried to stop me, but supported me wholly. The most difficult thing now is that the grandchildren don't get to see their grandmother and their relatives. I have a large family in Sweden; I grew up with cousins and we got together every summer. I can't give my children that when I live here. That is too bad, because they have quite a few cousins their age in Sweden. I try to visit there as much as I can, but it is not as often as I would like. When you are a family of four, it is a bit more difficult. Last year I went by myself with my son. It was the first time and it worked out really well. When they get a little older, I suppose that I will take one or both of them for visits there. After having emigrated, I sometimes start thinking that if I lived in Sweden, I would see my relatives a lot more because I lived so close to them. But I don't know if it is just a fantasy that I have, or if it would really be like that if I lived there. When I lived in Gothenburg, my father lived a short distance outside the city. Perhaps it took ten minutes by car to get there, or you could bicycle to his place in fifteen or twenty minutes, but we did not see each other that often even though we were so close.

I speak nothing but Swedish to my children. My wife

did not like that initially—her family was here and I spoke Swedish with my son and they did not understand what I said. She thought it was impolite. I suppose it was to a certain degree, but now I think she sees the value in it, because they can speak Swedish fluently now even if speaking English is easier. Most Americans think it is enormously positive that I speak Swedish with my children. They learn another language when they are small. They have been to Sweden. They get to learn something about Swedish culture—all this is kept alive. I don't know how many times I have heard people say: "My parents were Swedish. As a child I remember hearing them speaking Swedish, but neither of them taught me." I find that a pity.

When you come from Sweden and see the discrimination towards immigrants there, you feel that you have it really good in the United States. I have to remember that I am an immigrant here. I was not born here, but most consider me an American. To be an immigrant in Sweden would be very difficult. I can understand how difficult it would be to move from southern Europe to Sweden. It is like moving to the moon. In many ways you have to admire how a lot of the immigrants manage it. Many of them pretend that they are Swedes and like Swedish culture, but they come from countries where everything is so different— social interaction, openness, how you behave, how things are done. Then to move to Sweden, to put on a down jacket and winter boots, to not say a word—that must really be difficult. If I were a foreigner in Sweden and only spoke my native language with my children, most Swedes would probably think that was unbelievably unpleasant.

When my wife studied Swedish for immigrants, there were highly educated people from other countries who did not have a chance to get equally good jobs in Sweden. In how many Swedish companies do you see a CEO who speaks Swedish with a heavy accent? If I had come from Greece to Sweden, I would probably have ended up cleaning the toilets at the central train station. At my current job I think there are more individuals who were not born in the United States than were born here. On many internal meetings, with ten people around the table, two might be Americans. The others come mostly from Europe, but also from Asia and India.

To be an immigrant in the United States, especially if you come from Europe, is more positive than negative. People are interested. Most people here have some connection to Europe, and they want to learn more about it. But what Americans know about Europe is still not very good. When I moved here, I thought that Americans were so uneducated; they knew so little about the rest of the world. But when you live here, you begin to understand why—the United States is such an incredibly large country and there is so much to learn. They have a short history with many wars and they have built up this country in a very, very short time. In addition, the United States is sort of isolated from the rest of the world. There are great distances to other countries with the exception of Mexico and Canada. So I supposed it is easy to become focused on oneself. When I lived in Sweden, I always knew what was going on in other parts of the world. Now I feel that I have no clue about what goes on outside the United States. If you really want it, that information is available, but in some way it does not seem that important any more.

Before we had children, when I traveled somewhere, I tried to extend my stay over a weekend, rent a car, drive around, or simply just go walking. It was very interesting. Because I have traveled that way, I think I have understood why Americans are so focused on the United States—you see many different cultures and so much variation within the US. Take New Orleans, for example. I have been there a couple of times, and the last time my wife came along. I was going to a trade show that started on a Monday, and we flew in on the Friday before and stayed over the weekend—our first time without the children. We went just to look around. There are many influences from France. We who live in Oregon think that we know what "American" is. But when you come to a place like New Orleans, the values are not the same. It is like going to a completely foreign country. For that reason it would be fun to just travel around and see the entire United States. You realize that there really is no real reason for Americans to go abroad—to discover the United States takes a lifetime.

I really missed Sweden a great deal during the early years—the first five years maybe. I missed my family, Swedish holidays, Christmas, Midsummer, birthdays, all of that. When you live abroad and things get tough, you develop this idyllic notion of Sweden: *If I lived in Sweden this would not happen!* When things are rough, you automatically get homesick. When I first moved here, I had very little contact with Sweden. Sweden just disappeared. But now it is easy to get information through the internet and you can call almost as much as you want to. I have a lot more contact with Sweden now, so my need to move home has probably diminished. A lot of it has to do with me realizing that home might be here, even though I will always say that Sweden is home. It will not matter if I have lived here for sixty years, Sweden will always be home. I still have a few years left until I can say that I have lived half my life in the United States, but it is not that far off.

A lot of things have changed a great deal in Sweden too, so to a certain extent I feel like a stranger there. I would be an immigrant if I moved back. The people I knew do not keep in touch as much any more. They have changed, and I have changed a lot too. Having lived somewhere else for so long has left a mark on me. I don't think like a Swede any more—I notice that when I go back home for a vacation. Last summer the entire family went to Sweden and I noticed then how American I had become. For example, I no longer understand the Swedish health care system. My son suddenly became very ill the first night in Skövde, and my wife thought that he had a case of whooping cough. In the morning we tried get in to see a doctor. We could not even reach a doctor, because they only answered the telephone on Tuesdays, and it was not Tuesday. After spending several hours on the phone, I called a taxi and took my son to the hospital emergency room. There I was told that they did not have a pediatrician, so they refused to see him. From there we continued on to a children's health center where they could not see him for several hours. But they did have time for all the bureaucratic requirements and they made a plastic card for him. On top of it all, it cost 1800 Swedish *kronor*, about three times as expensive as a doctor's visit in Oregon. There are no private doctors in Skövde. When my children get sick in Portland, they get to come in and see a doctor the same day—without exception.

Right now we have no plans to move back. When our son was born, we had to decide if we wanted him to attend a Swedish school or an American school. At that point we were very close to moving back to Sweden. I applied for a job at Ericsson and flew over to Sweden for an interview. They offered me the job, but then, when we started discussing my salary, it was the last time I seriously thought about moving back. I would be paid about 30% of what I make in the United States! That was a pretty major step down, when you consider the fact that taxes are higher in Sweden. But that was not the only deciding factor. We also considered that we—here in the United States—with the kind of job I had, could afford having my wife stay at home to take care of the children. We can afford a house; we can live in place where we like to live; we can have the things we want. We have a great deal of freedom.

So when I looked at what I would earn in Sweden, and on the kind of freedom we would have there, we would have lost a great deal. When I realized what kind of housing I would be able to afford, we would end up somewhere on the outskirts of Stockholm. I would have to commute, my wife would have to go to work, and the children would have to be in daycare all day. That was not a lifestyle we wanted. We thought that it was worth a lot that she could stay home with the children. We did not want to force the children out of bed early in the morning, drive them to daycare for an entire day to be raised by others. Before I emigrated, we lived in Högsbohöjd, a large apartment complex in Gothenburg. People stole our laundry. People urinated and defecated in the stairways. Apartments were burglarized. I could not imagine moving back just to end up in that again! Sure, we could afford something better, buy a house or a row house somewhere, but then I would be a slave to that. We already have everything here. Our quality of life would go down considerably, and that made us decide to stay put. If we could have kept the quality of life and freedom that we have here, we would have considered moving to Sweden. The freedom we have, the financial freedom here, is worth a lot. Ours might not be a luxurious life, but at least we have possibilities here. We can choose. There are also many couples here where both choose to work, but that is their choice.

I heard a Swedish woman say how degrading it is for a woman to cook and be a stay-at-home mom. I think that people in Sweden have lost a sense of what life is all about. I work—not my wife—because I have the highest income potential. I work in high tech and my wife's education is in languages. That is not the result of gender roles—I would actually rather stay at home with the children if I could. My wife does not stay at home in order to serve me. She does her share of the work and I do mine in order for the children to have a good home and a central place in life where they feel a sense of belonging. And we raise our children ourselves. We think that is important, but I believe many Swedes have forgotten that completely. I don't know if Swedes use that as a defense because they have ended up in that situation: they defend themselves by saying that it is degrading to stay home with the children. To stay at home with the children—it was common that women did that during the 40s, 50s, and to a certain degree into the 60s—has for some reason become something negative in Sweden and in certain parts of the United States as well. But I think people here have realized that raising your own children, instead of having a day care person do it, is not something negative. If you have two children, there will be ten years that you have to dedicate to them. After that, you can do other things. Raising your own children is something you can choose to do; we can make that choice in the United States.

When I came to the United States, I did not look for social interaction with other Swedes. I really don't know why. When I was here as an exchange student, I stayed away from Swedes. I was here for a year to learn English and get to know the culture. I was not here to speak Swedish or spend time with Swedes. I thought that I was lucky that I came to a place where there were no other Swedes. There were some other students from South America at the school, three or four of them, and they were always together. They became isolated, or isolated themselves, because they walked around as a group speaking Portuguese or Spanish to each other: they never entered into American life. Later, when we moved to Oregon, I don't think I actively looked for Swedes, but I see Swedes and I have Swedish friends.

I don't think I observed that many Swedish traditions when I moved here. For Christmas I try to make it as Swedish as possible: Swedish Christmas songs, rice pudding, ginger snaps, smorgasbord. It might not be much more than that. I try to take the things I like from Sweden and mix them into my everyday life here. The language is important since every single relative on my side of the family lives in Sweden, and the youngest of them do not speak English, and neither do my maternal grandparents. So for me it is important that my children learn Swedish, and if they would like to move there, they have that option. If they do not learn Swedish, it will be hard, if not even impossible, for them to move there. I speak English with my wife, we always have, and speaking Swedish is becoming more and more difficult for her.

When I want Swedish food, I cook it myself. I make Swedish pancakes or bake Swedish coffee buns. The

only thing I can't do is soft coffee breads. My mother
makes a soft coffee bread that is simply fantastic. I have
to travel to Sweden to get that. Other than that, if we
feel like it, we can prepare anything we want. The need
to eat Swedish food might have been more pressing the
first couple of years, then it was no longer important to
have it every day. We always have Swedish crisp bread
at home. The things I miss, like Swedish cheeses and
Marabou chocolate, you can buy here now. You can
go to IKEA and buy caviar and soft whey-cheese. And
Swedish butter knives! I don't notice them myself, but
when Americans come to visit, they probably see a lot of
Swedish things in our house.

I think I have revised my view of the United States a
great deal. When I first came, I had such an idyllic view
of the United States, and I thought that it was like the
movies. Then I realized that there is an everyday life here,
too. I went through this whole process of weaning myself from Sweden and getting accustomed to the United
States. Even if Oregon and Washington are very similar
to Sweden, I realized, after having lived here for a while,
that they are also very different—the way houses look, the
way blocks are divided. After a while, either you accept it
or you don't. I arrived here with my Swedish set of values,
then came to understand that many of them really have
nothing to do with the United States. They are not valid
here; they do not match. Here, the discussions are completely different; the assumptions are different; you build
on a different kind of foundation. The way I think—about
politics, morality, work, my rights and responsibilities—
changed dramatically over time. When I visit Sweden, I
notice how much I have changed. It is difficult to under-

stand rent subsidies and child subsidies. These are discussions I no longer enter into.

When I first came to the United States, I thought that life was good as long as you made money, but if you didn't make money things could become very difficult. At that time I did not really make that much money myself. To be unemployed—I think less and less about that now that I have become established here, that I have a decent income and have a good life. If I lose my job, I can always get a new one somewhere. You don't have to pity yourself and wait for the government to send you money. Here you take any kind of job, even if that means working for McDonald's or some store while you look for the kind of work you normally do. You can always make money, but you might have to figure out for yourself how you are going to do it.

In the United States it is not one hundred percent true that you can do anything you want to, simply because you want to, but you have many more possibilities here.

I suppose this attitude attracted me: if I wanted something, I had to go out and get it myself. The county will not send a taxi for you to ride in. All of this is not entirely positive either; everything has a flip side. Americans pay a little bit too much attention to themselves, and not enough on the bigger picture. That is one of the more negative aspects: most things are focused on short-term thinking or the micro level, instead of the macro level. For example, take something like transportation: if you are going to build a light rail system, you can't just look at the cost of laying the tracks, and if the cost will be paid back in two or three years. There will also be less pollution and so on. I think there should be more of this kind of thinking in the United States.

When I moved here, there were many things I did not know anything about, like saving for your retirement. I did not have a clue. When I started working here, I did not save any money in a pension fund, but after a couple of years I began to realize that it was probably pretty important. I suppose I thought that I would not stay here that long; I was not used to thinking like that. There is no governmental entity that keeps an eye on this and to which you can make an appeal. Instead you have to do this entirely on your own. I also didn't know that you can sue individuals, and that someone can sue you for millions of dollars if their kid happens to hurl himself through your window. That you always have to think about things like this, is the most negative aspect of the possibilities you have.

What I miss is my Swedish family, little things in everyday life that we did together as a family. Just seeing each other and spending time together—not big things really. Personally I would not mind spending a couple of months in Sweden every year, but I don't think I could convince my wife to go along with that. It has nothing to do with Sweden, but more with this thing of visiting the same place year after year. I don't think she minds going to Sweden— she is just tired of Skövde. It is a typical, small, Swedish town, and if you have been there once, you have seen it. I can understand her.

Sometimes I wonder: *What would have happened if I had not moved to the United States?* My life would have been so different. If I had stayed in Sweden, if I had done the same things that most Swedes do, my life would not have become as good as the one I have here. Early on, I think my mother saw the difference between the United States and Sweden more clearly than I did. She never put any pressure on me to move back home. I even think that she—to a certain extent—wanted me to stay in the United States, because she realized that I would have a much better life here than I could have in Sweden.

X

COMING BACK WAS A SHOCK

Maria (b. 1957)

Gothenburg, Sweden, 1998

I think curiosity makes you want to go abroad. For me it began as an *au pair* in England, but I had felt a desire to go somewhere even before that. I hadn't done very much traveling in my life, because as a child we only went "home," as we called it, to Finland and my father's childhood home. We visited my grandparents. After that there was not enough vacation and money left for anything else. So I had not been outside Scandinavia until I managed to get out into the world myself, and I thought England was so incredibly exciting. It whetted my appetite.

I moved to the United States with my husband in June, 1983. When we moved from Sweden, we never said "Now we're leaving Sweden forever," but we formally left Sweden and did not maintain a domicile here. I was in the middle of my education when we moved, and I asked for a deferment for a year or two. So somehow I thought that alright: *I can do this for two years.* Before you leave, you think two years is a long time.... We had gotten married the same year, and our wedding was very hastily arranged. This sounds unromantic, and was the result of a technicality. It was a question of obtaining a residency visa. My husband had something called an L-1 visa, and I received something called L-2. This meant that I could stay in the United States as long as I remained married to him. I did not have a personal work permit. My husband went over with a Swedish company, which had started a subsidiary in the United States.

We had visited the United States a few years earlier, the same year Mt. St. Helens erupted. When we flew from Vancouver to Seattle, they made an extra turn around the volcano and pointed out the crater. The top still smoldered then. We traveled partly as a result of my husband's work—the company already had close contacts with a Portland firm—and we also had Swedish friends who lived in Vancouver, Canada. But we traveled across the entire United States—spent a week in Boston; saw New York City; flew to Hawaii; drove Highway 101 from Los Angeles to San Francisco.

So I came to the United States with my husband, but I had a great urge to travel myself. It was the adventure that beckoned. I suppose I have always felt guilty towards my mother, because I was pregnant with my first child—her first grandchild—and we moved on my mother's birthday. That was a hard thing to do to her, and I know that she suffered. But they were so brave, my parents, and they have tried to maintain a good attitude and be positive about it. The way they put it was this: If I had not gone, they would never have made it over to the United States. So in a way they have gotten something out of it too. It wasn't easy for my mother since she is afraid of flying. I don't know what's behind it, but many Swedes say that they don't want to visit the US, and I think my mother belongs to that group. I suppose my parents had been pumped full of the worst propaganda from the Swedish media, and they were really positively surprised on their first visit. They really were! They had a completely different notion of what the United States was than what they experienced in Oregon.

I felt, as I mentioned, a little bit guilty about leaving Sweden, but most of all it was exciting. And I was so tired because we had been busy with all the preparations. It had been very stressful before our departure, and it was so wonderful just to sit down on the plane. Because the move was taken care of and paid for by the company, we took advantage of it and brought quite a lot. We did not have that much, so we ran around IKEA and bought a big bed among other things. Because we were going to move abroad, I remember that we could buy everything tax free. Another Swede, who had a Portland connection, took care of the move, and a moving company came to our apartment and packed all our things.

We had no problems at all with immigration and customs when we came to Seattle—it wasn't like landing in New York on our first trip a couple of years earlier. That was tough! So my experience was that New York was more difficult than Seattle. We were met by a Swede from the company who had recently married an American woman. What surprised me the most was that she, who was my age, practically rushed up to me, pulled up my hand to inspect my wedding ring. It was so funny, typically American, because it is so important to American women what size diamond you have: "*I want a big one in my ring!*" Is size seen as a measurement of love, or is it just the amount of money he has spent on her? All of this was completely alien to me. I had learned a new Swedish word only the week before—*alliansring**—the traditional way to do an engagement ring and a wedding ring. I did not know that before. I had a bad cold when we went to the jeweler, and we just picked something. That was how important it was to me. And then I came to the United States and was completely inundated by a bunch of questions and a great deal of curiosity about my wedding ring. It was so strange—something of a cultural shock.

When we arrived in Portland, a Swedish couple who worked for the company but who were on vacation in Sweden at the time, lent us their apartment. While they were gone, we could look around and find a place of our own. We arrived in the United States on June 5, the day before Sweden's National Day. On my first morning in the United States I remember that I unpacked a small wooden Swedish flag pole that my husband's parents had given us, and put it on the table because it was June 6th.

I thought that we would be gone for a year or two, but I had not set a time limit. I did not know. The subsidiary in the United States was established—at least this is how I understood it—because it would be a fun thing for the employees in Sweden to be able to go the United States for a year or two. An adventure. So that's how I saw it, but this might be a reconstruction.

I spoke English fairly well when I came to the United

---

* Commonly called "eternity rings" in English, these rings are studded with diamonds or white sapphires.

States, and my husband relied on me, because he was more cautious and felt a bit more lost in the language. I had worked as an *au pair* in England and had already forced myself over that threshold where you dare to speak. So I became the one who had to call everywhere and fix everything because he was too embarrassed to speak. For example, before calling the utility company, I prepared myself by taking some time to write everything down first, and looking up words in the dictionary. My English wasn't any better than that. In addition, I was pregnant and did not know any of that terminology. I had doctor's appointments and had to learn words like *uterus* and many other words I had never heard before. You had to know what "German measles" were and things like that. All my experiences with doctor's visits and the like were very positive; they went well. On the other hand I have nothing to compare with, but I am very satisfied.

All our insurance policies were supposed to have been handled by the company, but our entire American residency evolved into one great collision with reality. I was naïve and gullible when we moved to the United States, and believed what people said to me, but my American experience taught me the exact opposite: Never believe that anything turns out the way they say; never trust anyone. It started when my husband's company was bought by another company in Stockholm, which then suddenly decided that it did not want to keep the US subsidiary. We had a beautiful contract when we left and I felt very secure and satisfied. We had been guaranteed two trips back home annually; the childbirth expenses were to be covered; there was even a retirement plan for me—everything was really top notch. It was a very good package. Then my great sense of security was immediately overthrown. It began the first week when my husband did not get the job he came over for. He went to the interview and did not get the job. And his boss left on his honeymoon to Sweden.

Perhaps it was a cultural thing that lay behind my husband not getting the job. Later we heard that you could not go to a job interview dressed the way my husband had done—in jeans and tennis shoes. I sulked and my husband sulked: jeans and tennis shoes? That was not really what he had worn at all, we thought. He had worn a pair of grey jeans, which is not really the same thing as blue jeans, a coat, and Ecco shoes—which might have looked like tennis shoes to an American. We had just arrived and did not know these dress codes. But you are supposed to look more traditional, preferably a dark suit and tie and black shoes. He probably looked more like a teenager or a rocker. In retrospect, I see that it really could have had something to do with the clothes. I don't know what the chemistry between them was like, of course, and what his body language conveyed. He is good at what he does, but something went wrong. So there we were: alone in a new country, our furniture on the Atlantic, a baby on the way, and forced vacation. *What should we do?*

At the same time that this happened, things started to fall apart in the Swedish company. Promises and agreements were up in the air, and for a while we did not even know if the birth was going to be covered. That's how it began, and then it sort of continued along the same lines. Well, in the end things worked out. The company got other projects instead and did well for a couple of years, but then new problems emerged. One of my husband's colleagues from that time is dead now; he disappeared in his airplane without a trace in the Bermuda triangle. They have still not found him or his plane. Two of the other Swedes definitely wanted to return home; their wives especially pushed hard for it. Then they got tired of always having to hunt for new jobs and not knowing when a project would be over and what would come after that; that is the disadvantage of being a consultant. But I was not that involved in all of this because we had bought a house in Beaverton, and I took care of that and stayed home with the children. Life is busy when the children are young.

One difficult aspect of life had to do with authorities and insurance: we did not know where to turn or who we could trust. There were so many things you had to take care of yourself. You had to read through something that basically was an estimate, and it was like a jungle trying to figure out what was most advantageous and what was offered at the best price. I felt that was harder in America. Neither did I have the necessary language for this. Actually that was true for a number of situations: when you wanted to discuss specific things and were unable to express yourself a bit more nuanced and intelligently; when there was something technical you wanted to buy. Take the word "appliance" for example; we don't really have that word in Swedish. We say *vitvaror*, but I think that you can't really translate that word. It took a while before I understood what "appliances" were. In those situations I felt like a real yokel.

Being a Scandinavian among Americans, I fell on fertile ground. They were interested and positive. Of course, they asked about Swedish drinking habits, and some asked— and this is actually true!—if there were polar bears on the streets. Some people asked if we had telephones in Sweden.

Being Swedish in the United States was something positive for me, and I just don't mean people interacting with a positive attitude—it also gave me a kind of perspective on my life. Here, in Sweden, I am nobody, but there I was Swedish! It made me a little bit interesting and special—and I don't mean to suggest that I was remarkable. But it gave me something extra beyond the ordinary. Here I am Swedish, but everyone else is too. Obviously I have taken my unique American experience home with me, but it is not as well received here to tell people that you have lived in the United States. For many people it is, but sometimes I feel that I really should keep quiet about it. They might see it as boasting, or that it suggests that something is missing in their own lives. They don't have the energy to listen; it is too much. There is no interest, no follow-up questions, nothing at all. All you get is: "Well, so what? What do you think you are?" I feel that this is how they think. I don't know if they are envious or what it is—perhaps they think that you are trying to make yourself important. So you have to be very careful about telling people. Naturally, there are those who say: "Wow, what an experience," but they are the exceptions.

In Portland we spoke Swedish at home, of course, and I always spoke Swedish with the children even if we were out doing things together. Sometimes this was very fortunate, as when they spontaneously would blurt out: "*Titta vilken tjockis!*" [Look at that fat person!] or something like that. Then I was really grateful that this was said in Swedish. Sometimes I got angry at Swedish friends in America when they—in various social situations with Americans—kept chattering in Swedish. I think that is so inconsiderate. It might be American wives of Swedish men who must have felt really excluded, even if they were nice and polite and said: "Just go on speaking Swedish. It is so much fun to listen to." But after several years of that, listening to Swedish could not have been that much fun in social situations. It is a question of showing some consideration: sometimes I felt speaking English among Swedes was necessary.

I am sure it was good that we spoke Swedish at home— we did not feel all that homesick. Because I knew this from my experience in England, it was so wonderful to meet a Swede occasionally and just be able to babble on. I can imagine that someone who is married to an American really gets a lot of pleasure from the Swedish gatherings and Swedish friendships. We took Sweden with us in some way. Eventually speaking English took over more and more between me and the children, because the older they got, the more often they had friends over. I had an experience related to this when I was a child myself. I had a girlfriend whose parents came from Finland, and when I visited her, her parents always spoke Finnish to her. I did not understand any of it, and you start thinking that they are talking about you, and you feel excluded and become vulnerable. I thought about this when we had Americans visiting our house; consequently I spoke a fair amount of English with my children at home as well.

After a few years, the fact that we were so far away from my parents and my sisters started to bother me. Initially everything was just exciting, and I wrote letters describing it all. It was an adventure, and when we visited back in Sweden, it was still just a lot of fun. On the other hand—suddenly thirteen years had passed by and my children had begun to grow up. Then this feeling came: *Are they going to become Americans? Will we never live a bit closer to our family in Sweden and see each other a bit more spontaneously?* I suppose I had a desire to experience that too. Sweden is home, after all. This is where you fit in, where you really are your true self. At least you tell yourself that you know where people stand, that you know the rules. In some way it feels more secure and easier to handle. America was more exotic and was—even after 13 years—more of an adventure.

I never considered, for example, becoming an American citizen. I really don't know why. Was there some part of me that knew that I would one day move from there? I suppose I felt like a visitor, never like an American. I had a green card, so I had a work permit and all the rights except the right to vote, but since I am not that politically involved, not being able to vote did not matter very much. The whole issue of keeping one's Swedish citizenship has to do with the fact that people in our generation are able to keep a foot in two different countries. Those who moved in earlier times saw emigrating, I think, as something much more definitive. They really made an effort to become Americans. I have heard that they did not encourage people to speak their native language, and for the children it was important to lose their accent to get assimilated as quickly as possible.

All my children were born in the United States, and they have both Swedish and American citizenship. I hope that the years there gave them broader horizons and a deeper perspective than if they had not had that experience. At the same time, having lived there is not without complications. I am sure that they feel—at least partly— what I feel: *You call two countries home and that when you are in one country, you long for the other. You often compare the two and find it hard to decide which is better.* I think this is especially true for my oldest boy who feels that a dual citizenship is complicated at times. Otherwise I think that children, compared to us adults, have a much greater ability to really be in the present. Now my children have slipped into their Swedish world wonderfully well, and are completely busy with school, friends, and activities. In other words, now it is Sweden that matters. But they definitely want their father to stay in the same house in Oregon. It is their childhood home and they want to be able to go there and visit.

That first year in the United States we flew back home twice, because the trips were paid for. All in all we went back seven times during those thirteen years, but initially we travelled more frequently. There was a seven-year stretch when I did not visit Sweden at all. I never went by myself, and once we all went together. I primarily went to Sweden to visit my mother and father, and to see friends I had here. Sometimes my parents took the children so that we could have some vacation on our own. Once we went to Denmark, and once we sailed through the *Göta kanal.*† We also had visitors regularly from Sweden; both my parents and my husband's parents visited three or four times each. All my siblings came over to United States and a few friends did as well. In the beginning especially, I felt that we had visitors from Sweden almost all the time. Our neighbor thought that we should call ourselves a hotel, because we always had a guest. When people travel that far,

---

† A waterway consisting of a series of lakes and canals, completed in 1832, that connects Stockholm on the Baltic with Gothenburg on the North Sea.

they like to stay a while too. It was really a lot of fun initially, but going to look at Multnomah Falls for the fiftieth
time got a bit tiring.

We had a lot of contact with other Swedes and Scandinavians in Portland, and in many ways we had our own
"Little Sweden" on top of that. I was not active in a church
or religious organization, but I participated in the Lucia
celebrations[‡] every year so that the children would know
what Lucia was and learn a few Christmas songs. Every
year we participated in a program for the children, and I
helped with games and bought bags of candy for the children's party at the end of Christmas. That was all done
in the traditional Swedish way. Early on I also became
involved with the group of women called "The Sewing
Circle." Originally, some Swedish women just sent out
personal invitations to their friends, but it was an unspo-
ken rule that if you had met a new Swedish woman, it was
OK to invite her along to this coffee drinking gathering.
There was a Swedish woman who had lived in California
and had been a member of SWEA, the Swedish Women's
Educational Association. She thought that we should start
a SWEA group in Portland, and we met to discuss this.
But it turned out that everyone in Portland wanted to take
it easy. No one wanted to take on additional work or have
a more organized type of gathering with a president, fundraising, and everything else that would come with it. So
this idea petered out. On the other hand we decided that
instead of one person having to invite everyone over and

---

‡ Swedes celebrate Lucia on the 13th of December. The Lucia bride
is dressed in a white gown, wearing a crown of lights—real or electric
candles—on her head.

do all the baking, we would form a club where the host would not have to bake. The guests would bake. And everyone would be welcome. In this way, the gatherings became a little bit less personal and more like an organization, but still very unpretentious. Initially we got together every other month. People could sign up on an address list and throw in some money for postage and a map to the next meeting place. And if somebody had a special news item from Sweden, or a suggestion that would interest everyone, it might also be included in the mailing. People got more and more excited about this, and I know that they meet every month now.

If I were to describe the Swedes I met in the United States, I would call them *oddballs*. I am probably one myself too, and it is something I have thought about occasionally. Many have a slightly crazy streak, a great deal of energy. I suppose there is a certain type of person who packs up and leaves, just as there is another type who does not. At the time I was about to leave, we had a school reunion, and when I mentioned that I was pregnant and on my way to the United States, some just about fell over backwards. "How can you leave Mölnlycke?" and "Are you going to have a baby without your mother?" I think it takes a certain kind of curiosity and courage to leave.

I found the Christmas holidays in Oregon good, except for the weather, which was sometimes quite dreary. The tulips were almost in bloom, it was dark and wet, and a plastic Santa Claus blinked on the neighbor's roof. I did not like that very much. Previously I had only celebrated Christmas at my mother's, and now, for the first time in my life, I had the pleasure of being in charge of Christmas myself. We always had guests and a Christmas table in our home, and both Swedes and Americans came. Introducing our American guests to Swedish Christmas dishes and Swedish traditions always put me in good spirits. It was also very important for me to try to recreate for my children what I had experienced myself. For me, traditions felt more important there than they do here in Sweden. I felt more Swedish there than I do here. This year, I feel that Christmas doesn't really matter.

What I found most exciting about life in America was to meet new people and see new places, to discover and experience. The feeling of being independent and able to support ourselves was also important. Initially, when the children were small, I was a stay-at-home mom, but later I started working. I suppose my first real job was with a business we started that had to do with crayfish. The crayfish business was just an idea that grew out of our own attempts to maintain Swedish traditions, among them the crayfish parties. When we fished crayfish and discovered how nice and tasty they were, we had the idea that we ought to be able to sell them in Sweden. They were just like Swedish crayfish, and they were big too. I wasn't involved initially; it was my husband and an American who started it. Later I was asked to help out—the first time was when the crayfish were going to be cooked—and then I suppose I became indispensable. They would never have been able to pull it off without help. The crayfish turned out to be a much bigger thing than we had initially anticipated, and everything took a lot of time. My husband did not have time for all of it, so it became my responsibility. I was the one who received the catch, weighed it, and paid for it. I found help when we needed it. I did all the practical stuff: cooked them, packaged them, froze them, drove them to the freezer, and kept track of everything. It was seasonal work—June, July and August, into September sometimes, and I did it for four years.

During the last two years the work changed. One of the changes was that we made a deal with a crab cooker who both had the equipment and the personnel. I was there the first year and made the brine, tasted every batch and oversaw the packaging, but after that they managed on their own. Another change was that we stopped exporting to Sweden. Part of this change had to do with a disagreement with our Swedish buyer, part of it was that new EU rules would require so much more from us—approved facilities and increased costs. Instead we decided to sell only within North America: to IKEA stores in Canada and the US, to Swedish clubs, organizations, consulates, to others who wanted to have crayfish parties. I would probably never have applied for a job like that, but it was fun because you had the feeling that the business was your own.

I also worked in a gambling café called Dotty's; it was a chain that had storefronts in several shopping malls. Each place had approximately ten café tables and six video poker machines. People came to gamble, and were lured in, just as in Las Vegas, with free coffee, tea, and soft drinks. And they could buy very cheap fast food like sandwiches, hamburgers, hot dogs, fruit and yogurt. There was no hard liquor served, but people could buy wine and beer. You had to be 18 years old to enter. My job was to serve food and handle the coupons that were used to play Keno. They were good for ten minutes, and sometimes they almost did not make the last game. It could become very hectic. The salary was low, but the tips were good—when people won they got so happy that they could give you a 20 dollar tip. Sometimes I would be confronted with a few sad and slightly angry individuals who did not want to go home, but wanted to stay and win back what they had lost. I handled a whole lot of money. Because I worked alone, it was a bit worrisome to cross a huge, desolate parking lot late at night. It was a relief quitting that job. I had taken that job just so that I could pay for a ticket to Sweden when my mother turned 60.

During my last year in the United States, I worked as a waitress in a lunch restaurant. It was busy and great. There, too, tips made up most of my income. I started working at eleven and was done at three, and I could eat anything on the menu. And I got money in my pocket right away, the day's tips; it was really instant gratification that gave a great sense of satisfaction. It was a wonderful place, well run and great coworkers. I liked that place a lot.

When my husband and I split up, there were practical and economic reasons for me to move back to Sweden. In addition, it was a question of family—both my parents are alive, my sisters live here as do my children's cousins. It would be nice to live close to them. I have to admit that it felt somewhat strange to consider a move somewhere in the United States. America is a place without roots to me; moving felt totally wrong: *So, where shall I move now? I think I'll move to San Francisco.* That's simply not possible. I think I need to feel some kind of connection to the place where I settle down. And I did not have a job that took me somewhere. I could have considered that—moving for the sake of a job. In my case family relationships became the determining factor, but the security that Swedish society could offer, and which I needed at that point in my life, was also important. I saw trying to make it as a single mother in the United States as much tougher and more frightening. I think I would have had to work day and night with the children living with their father. That was the vision I had. I would have considered staying in the United States if I had been childless and free from worry about their well-being. You can take care of yourself—I believe that.

The custody question was not an issue for us, because the children's father thought that it was a good thing that they would grow up in Sweden and maybe spend the rest of their lives there. But you don't know how long this will last. Anyway, he viewed it positively that I moved here. That made things very simple in this regard. Officially, we have equal custody of the children, so he is not in any way shut out of their lives. The children went back to stay with him for a month last summer. I think things turned out OK, but they were happy to come back here too, and it really warmed my heart that they saw Sweden as home.

So I suppose it was really an obvious decision to move back to Sweden, but it took a while for me to admit it and realize that this was the case. I was very confused at that time—looking into things, trying to envision how I could make it in the United States, learning what the possibilities were. I became somewhat disillusioned when I thought about work, income, and having a place to live. I saw this nightmare scenario: two jobs and no time with the children. In addition to that, I wanted to leave; I did not want any ongoing economic involvement with my ex-husband. If I had stayed, we would have remained tangled up together with money and the children. This is a clearer situation; it is cleaner and calmer this way.

Everything started with us telling the children that we would get divorced, and that we might move. That turned out to be the worst thing for them—the thought of moving. The divorce itself turned out to be a detail. What was important to them was that they would have to move out of their home. "Can't Dad just keep an apartment nearby?" They had some friends—having divorced parents is so common nowadays—where the parents lived on our street, but in separate houses, so that children could walk between the two. I pursued that idea for a while, that the best solution for the children would be that I remained in the house. But that was economically impossible.

Two and a half years ago I flew to Sweden for the summer with the children, and I was close to having a meltdown and simply jumping ship. At that point I seriously considered not returning from Sweden, but I felt that I could not do that to the children. I had to go back and take care of things calmly and methodically. They must be given the chance—no matter how sad it would be—to be notified of this and have the opportunity to say goodbye. After that, I sort of took hold of the entire process. It took almost a full year. I told the children in February, and we moved in December. I kind of wanted to move that summer, but we did not get around to it. Everything gets so complicated. The children's father thought that there was so much to settle and agree on. At the same time it is difficult to approach each other when the situation is tense. Some days are a bit nicer, and then you don't want to spoil them. In that way you are tossed between hope and confusion. Yes, it is really difficult. But once I told the children I felt that it was my decision. That it took a year was an appropriate amount of time for them, I think. Initially they were sad, and with tears in their eyes dramatically told neighbors and friends in February. Then they got a small reprieve since we did not manage to leave that summer. They still got to start school in the fall and go until Christmas. Then we left. Actually it worked out pretty smoothly.

We brought a three cubic yard container and a pallet that we nailed sides and a lid on. That was all I had—those two containers. Shoes, rubber boots, leather boots, coats for five people—you quickly fill those moving boxes. You own a lot more than you think of purely personal stuff like books, records, photos, things the children have made in school. Junk, really, in other words. Christmas decorations—it's crazy, but that's the kind of stuff you haul across the Atlantic! Those things that have emotional value were more important than the big things. Beyond them there was a table, a cabinet, a bed. It was all I had in the way of furniture, in addition to some pots and pans, plates, and other small household items.

Coming back was a shock initially. We immediately visited the children's school so that they would have an idea of where they would be going. In Sweden, Christmas break had not started when we came. There was snow and a snow ball fight in the corridor. We sat outside the principal's office and waited, and the ninth grade kids ran around trying to smash snow in each other's faces. Girls screamed and there was running around and snowballs. I thought it was total chaos. My daughter sat all curled up and said: "What are they doing, what are they doing?" It was something of a horrifying experience. I had to ask the principal about it: "Hmm, is this the way it is?" But she just shrugged her shoulders: "Oh, it is just the snow. It will soon be gone." Of course, it was especially dramatic because of the snow; school is not normally that wild, I suppose. But one thing that struck me was the attitude of the school children toward the adults—I did not like it. The school lacked discipline and manners. In the United States there were rules in the schools. Among other things we received a small booklet before they entered middle school which parents and students both had to sign, certifying that they had read through the rules. It was like a contract. There was not going to be any arguing about something if the school had reason to call home about something a student had done. You were supposed to know that you had actually agreed that they were not supposed to do that. I thought that was really good. Here there was a small sign on the wall in the school where it said:

> *Try not to fight*
> *Try to solve a conflict with words.*
> *Try not to run in the corridors.*

And I thought to myself: *Try? What the hell? What kind of message is that? If you can't do something, it's OK?* It's a language between adults and children that bends over backwards, a language where no one should show authority, where everyone is "hi there" and on a first name basis. In the United States the teachers had much more pride in their work and a clearer job definition. They were more professional. They had their role; they had some authority; they dressed up a little bit for work. And the students had to address them as "Mr." or "Ms." And even at the parent-teacher conferences in Oregon, I got the impression that the teacher's attitude toward parents was more like grown-up to grownup. They were professionals who presented their plan, discussed rules and objectives in a much more sensible way. Many of the Swedish teachers here don't have that sense of professionalism. It is so wishy-washy. "I feel that I don't want to deal with this any more." That's the way Swedish teachers talk, and that is not just a few. I am disappointed with the Swedish schools because I thought that the students actually got a better education here. I am not at all sure about that now.

We had friends who came to the United States when their children were about ten years old. They both immediately became the best students in their class. From that we drew the conclusion that Swedish students were far ahead of the American ones. That was the way it was a couple of years ago. But the United States has either tightened up their curriculum, or Sweden has slipped behind, because that is not that way now. Now my kids came from America and became the best students in their class. They are far ahead in math and language, and the teachers here mostly seem to focus on keeping order in the classroom. They have no time left over for the curriculum because they spend their time parenting children. That's a bit sad.

One thing I miss from America, even if many Swedes see it as something superficial, is that people say "Have a nice day," and things like that. You miss this when you never hear it. When the cashier at the Swedish grocery store just sits there and stares straight down, and you have to pack your own bag—which you have to buy first!—and no one helps you to carry it. Attitudes are much tougher here. A lot of people are always out walking here, because people more often travel by bus and train than in the United States. So you always run into people on pedestrian paths and sidewalks, and then you are supposed to look away. You don't say "Hello" to people you don't know. I still say "Hi" or "Good morning," because it is a human being that

I meet. There are those who answer, of course, but some look scared or give you a look suggesting that you are really weird. If I had lived in Sweden all my life, I might also have stared at the ground or turned away. I think I have become a little bit more extroverted or people-friendly. And my oldest son pointed out that if we had moved into a house in the United States, the neighbors would have come over with some cookies, presented themselves, and said "Welcome!" There is nothing like that here. In Sweden, people look at you from behind the curtains.

What I miss in Sweden is a basic, positive spirit—it is hard for me to put my finger on what it is exactly. Perhaps it is that Americans seem happier. The United States was more fun! All this gets complicated. At the same time I have to say that what is so easy about a Swede is, to use that English expression: "What you see is what you get." A Swede is a little bit more direct and maybe not always that polite. My American brother-in-law received a letter after a test he took here in Sweden, and it was direct: "You did not pass." Period. He would have liked to have it phrased more indirectly, and that is what is so positive about the United States, I suppose. People always consciously emphasize what is positive; they see the individual and they are happy about other people's successes. In Sweden you are more conscious of *jantelagen*—about taking people down a few notches, and pull those down who stick out too much. I think that is very obvious, and I miss the American attitude. At the same time, I don't like that American "*Oh Great!!! Oh Hi!!!*" very much. It is so artificial and I am glad I'm not exposed to it anymore. I used to say that inflation had crept into the words "you love and you hate"—for me they are such big words. So in some way

I think I am quite Swedish on the inside, and somewhere this Swedish notion of *lagom*, just right, feels pretty good. I also think that Swedes are not very good at giving compliments. As a woman in the United States you always heard people say things like "What a nice dress!" or "Oh, nice boots!" That's fun; that's just a basic human thing. Everyone enjoys hearing things like that. Here you only feel people's eyes, because no one says anything. I don't know if it is jealousy or not wanting to disturb someone. But no one seems to realize that you actually can—verbally—encourage another person. People simply do not do that to the same extent in Sweden.

When we had Swedish visitors in the United States, they thought that we had become so Americanized. I don't know why I did not ask them to be specific. I suppose they just sighed—it was so obvious. I did not understand what they meant exactly, but I think they referred to these somewhat nebulous things. In the US, there was such an abundance of everything. Here, everything you buy comes in smaller packages. Here, you put a teaspoon of jam on your pancake; my kids used a tablespoon in the United States. I think visiting Swedes reacted to things like that: Wow, a gallon-sized box of wine, or a gallon jug of milk! There, generosity could be afforded—or unconsciously slipped into. That was sensational or almost shocking to a Swede who was used to everything being tighter, smaller, and stingier.

Even a thing like everyday comfort was better in the United States. It is much more complicated to live in Sweden—just look at the store hours. Think about *Systembolaget*, the State Liquor stores—it is Friday and 47 seven people are lined up ahead of you. The stores are crowded, the isles narrow, and the selection poor. It makes you very frustrated when you are used to Safeway or Fred Meyer where the isles are wide, the shopping carts big, the parking lot huge, your groceries are bagged for you, and taken to your car. There are big signs in the store telling you in which aisle things are. In Sweden you run around as in a labyrinth looking for things; you bump into people; you can't find room for your shopping cart. Shopping here is damned hard work! On a Saturday morning you might sleep in, and then you realize that you have an errand to do—and oops, everything has already closed. Of course, you get used to it, but it was much easier in the United States. Whatever you wanted to do was possible: that was how it felt. Here there are lines, obstacles, and hurdles everywhere.

The children adjusted to Swedish life incredibly fast—much better than I had anticipated. I had envisioned something like a year of gloom, but it lasted two weeks! It took a bit longer for my oldest boy—the older you are, the more at home you feel; the more you know, the more sensitive you are. He has done very well socially and is satisfied and happy, but he is still the one who might shed a tear sometimes in the evening after going to bed. If something reminds him about the United States—if he receives an email from a friend there—he might ask questions like: "When are we going to go to the United States again? Will you come then too? Can I go to high school there?" He misses some teachers; he thinks that the school was better in the United States.

It is very clear to me that my children feel much safer in Sweden. To a large degree this is the result of the exaggerated talk in the United States about kidnappings and carjackings and things like that. The children heard so much about it. They heard it—even if I rarely said anything about it myself—from other parents and from friends. The result was: "No, you can't walk there on your own. I'll drive you. Will there be a parent there? I can't leave you alone." The children were agitated there, especially one of my daughters. She did not dare to do anything on her own. She did not dare to stay in the car and wait for me if I had to run into a store to get some milk. Here she really feels a different sense of security and will ride her bicycle even if it is dark outside, and she will walk to her girlfriend's. Children in Sweden go to many more places by themselves. People don't have that kidnapping worry here.

I feel at home in Sweden, but I don't have the feeling that "this is where I will live and this is where I will die." Initially, I suppose, I mostly noticed the things I experienced as negative, but I don't see that anymore. Everything has become softened; it is not at all as black and white anymore and that is surely a result of me having integrated, of me understanding things better. I no longer think that the school is as horrible as I thought initially. I have seen more of it now, and I have been to parent-teacher conferences and met the teachers, and the children are fully integrated. Now I can also see many advantages here; I have become more accepting; I am more used to things and I am probably better adjusted too.

I think the United States surfaces in my mind every day; I might associate to the landscape or think about someone. I can see moving there sometime as a possibility. Not that I would move there with my children, but perhaps one of them settles down there in the future and I would go there as a result of that. You never know! To what degree have they been imprinted by America? To what degree do they feel American? It is primarily my oldest son who is drawn to the US the most. We'll have to see what happens to his relationship with his father. *Naturally, if all my children end up there, I'll go there, too.* At least that is how it feels now. For my oldest son, the United States is home—what he longs for is the house where we lived. Our dog is still there—he still has his father, dog, house, and friends back there.

But when the children visited Oregon this summer, things didn't turn out quite as they had expected. My oldest son had envisioned how he would go skating with his rollerblades with this friend with whom he had always gone before. But he hardly saw this friend at all—he had started smoking and hanging out and did not go skating with rollerblades anymore. His other friends—these boys were two years older—had their drivers' licenses, and one of them had a girlfriend, and they spent all their time necking in her room. Playing with a water pistol wasn't possible anymore. It was good for my son to see this too. Even if he had stayed in Oregon, things would have changed. Groups of friends like this do dissolve, and people enter new phases of their lives, especially when some of the friends are a little older. Great changes occur in just a few years. I feel that change is something that my children really got to experience early in life, and I have calmly tried to instill in them that "life is change." Wherever you are, some kind of change will still occur.

I hope that I will go back to visit the United States; it's a question of money. Cannon Beach—I just can't imagine that I will never walk there again! Somehow I will return there, sometime. I would like to travel around the world; I am curious to see the whole world, but I have a very different kind of longing for Oregon because it was my home for 13 years—emotionally intense years when our family was created. I feel that I have "built" so much there, given birth to and raised my children, been part of their early schooling, created a social network. Because it happened to be that period of my life, I think it became so powerful. In many ways they were perhaps the happiest years of my life.

POSTSCRIPT

A conversation describing an individual's personal story inevitably becomes—at least to a certain extent—a portrait of a specific time. One should therefore keep in mind that all these conversations were recorded around the time of the new millennium. Returning to them as a translator ten years later made it very clear to me that while some things that pertains to the life of the Swedes in the area have changed—for example, IKEA arrived in Portland in 2007, and in 2008 the city's Swedish Consulate closed after almost one hundred years of operation—much also remains the same. A few words about some of my post-interview questions to the story-tellers are therefore probably in order.

One of the major events for these emigrants has been a change in Swedish law. Before 2001, Swedish citizens could not retain their native citizenship if they became a citizen of another country. But in that year, the law changed and dual citizenship was allowed. As was mentioned previously, at the time of the original interviews, only Tobbe had become a US citizen. All the other participants were still Swedish citizens living in the United States as permanent, resident aliens—except Maria, who had ended up moving back to Sweden. Today, all the participants—except Maria and Carin—have become US citizens.

Another very significant development for these immigrants has been the growth of the internet. Email and websites both existed when these interviews were completed, but the explosion of internet content has simply been mindboggling. Today one can read Swedish newspapers, listen to Swedish radio, watch Swedish television, make phone calls, contact Swedish government agencies, businesses, and so on. There are not enough hours in the day to take it all in, and keeping in touch with Sweden from the other side of the planet has become easier than it ever was.

All the narrators still live and work in the same general area today that they did ten years ago, except Peter, who currently does long-distance commuting from Portland to a job in California. All except one are still married to the same spouse. Of those who worked ten years ago, no one has retired. Most feel that their stories still basically reflect their view of Sweden and the United States, even if a few think that they would compare less and emphasize things differently today. The current reversal of economic fortunes for Sweden and the United States is not a factor that makes anyone consider moving back to Sweden. However, the perception of an increasingly religious and politically conservative United States does seem to negatively affect the feeling of being "at home" with this aspect of American life, and gives rise to thoughts of moving among the majority of the participants living in the United States. Still, many realize that *thinking* about moving and actually *doing* it, are two very different things. Where one chooses to live ultimately appears to be determined by the country where the children decide to live. No one feels overwhelmingly homesick, but many would like to spend more time in Sweden as retirement approaches, and quite a few have started thinking about buying a summer home there. Maria has still not visited the United States since she left twelve years ago, but it remains high on her wish list.

SELECTED BIBLIOGRAPHY

Ander, O. Fritiof. *The Cultural Heritage of the Swedish Immigrant: Selected References*. Rock Island, IL: Augustana College Library, 1956.

Aronson, Hugo J. and L. O. Brockman. *The Galloping Swede*. Missoula, MT: Mountain Press Publishing Co, 1970.

Austin, Paul Britten. *On Being Swedish*. Coral Gables, FL: Univ. of Miami Press, 1968.

Baily, Ronald T. *Frozen in Silver: The Life & Frontier Photography of P. E. Larson*. Athens, Ohio: Swallow Press and Columbus: University of Ohio Press, 1998.

Barton, H. Arnold. *Letters from the Promised Land: Swedes in America, 1840-1914*. Minneapolis, MN: University of Minnesota Press, 1975.

—. *A Folk Divided: Homeland Swedes and Swedish Americans, 1840 – 1940*. Carbondale, IL: Southern Illinois University Press, 1995.

Beijbom, Ulf, editor. *Swedes in America: Intercultural and Interethnic Perspectives on Contemporary Research*. Växjö: Svenska Emigrantinstitutet, 1993.

Bunce, Eda, editor. *Gold and Green Timber: A History of the Nils-Peter Hult Family, Colton, Oregon*. Winchester, OR: Blackberry Press, 1978.

Daun, Åke. *Swedish Mentality*. Pennsylvania State University Press, 1996.

Gradén, Lizette. *On Parade: Making Heritage in Lindsborg, Kansas*. Uppsala: Universitas Uppsaliensis, 2003. (Disseration)

Hasselmo, Nils, editor. *Perspectives on Swedish Immigration*. Chicago: Swedish Pioneer Historical Society, in association with the Univ. of Minnesota-Duluth, 1978.

Lago, Don. *On the Viking Trail: Travels in Scandinavian America*. Iowa City: University of Iowa Press, 2004.

Lindmark, Sture. *Swedish America, 1914-32: Studies in Ethnicity with Emphasis on Illinois and Minnesota*. Studia historica upsaliensia 37. Stockholm: Läromedelsförlagen, 1971.

Lindquist, Emory. *An Immigrant's American Odyssey: A Biography of Ernst Skarstedt*. Rock Island, IL: Augustana Historical Society, 1974.

Ljungmark, Lars. *Swedish Exodus*. Translated by Kermit B. Westerberg. The Swedish Pioneer Historical Society. Carbondale: Southern Illinois Univ. Press, 1979.

Nordström, Lars. *Sweden*. Portland, OR: Graphic Arts Publishing, 1990.

—. *Making It Home*. Portland, OR: Prescott Street Press, 1997.

—. *Swedish Oregon*, Portland, OR: Swedish Roots in Oregon Press, 2008.

Norlen, Arthur. *The Vanishing Immigrants*. New York, NY: Vantage Press, 1976.

O'Hearn, Margareta. *The Effects of Cultural Factors on Marital Satisfaction among Swedish-American Couples*, 1997. (Dissertation)

Peterson, Oscar E. *75 Years of the Valby Lutheran Church: Historical Glimpses of Lutheran Mission Work in Morrow County, 1886–1986*. Publisher unknown.

Rasmussen, Janet E. *New Land, New Lives: Scandinavian Immigrants to the Pacific Northwest*. Northfield, MN: Norwegian-American Historical Association, and Seattle: University of Washington Press, 1993.

Runblom, Harald and Hans Norman, editor. *From Sweden to America: A History of the Migration*. Minneapolis: University of Minnesota Press, 1976.

Strickland, Ron. *River Pigs and Cayuses: Oral Histories from the Pacific Northwest*. San Francisco: Lexikos, 1984.

Swanson, Alan. *Literature and the Immigrant Community: The Case of Arthur Landfors*. Carbondale and Edwardsville: Southern Illinois University Press, 1990.

Tingelstad, Gertrude. *Scandinavians in the Silverton Country: Their Arrival and Early Settlement*. Silverton, OR: Silverton Appeal Tribune, 1978.

Veirs, Kristina. *Nordic Heritage Northwest*. Seattle: The Writing Works, 1982.

Youngquist, Erick H. *America Fever: A Swede in the West 1914 – 1923*. Nashville: Voyageur Publishing Co, Inc, 1988.

About Lars Nordström

*Lars Nordström, born and raised in Stockholm, Sweden,
has lived in Oregon 1978–1981, and since 1984.*

Lars Nordström was born in 1954 in Stockholm, Sweden, where he lived until 1974. He was educated at the University of Stockholm and Portland State University in Portland, Oregon, where he received a BA in English in 1981. He then moved to Uppsala University, Sweden, where he received his Ph.D. in American literature in 1989. He is the recipient of several Fulbright grants, a Scandinavian Foundation grant for academic research in the USA, several Swedish Institute grants and awards, several Baltic Centre residency fellowships, as well as a Rockefeller Foundation Bellagio Center fellowship. His memoir *Making It Home* won an Oregon Book Award in 1998, and in 2008 his historical volume *Swedish Oregon* received the ASF Niskanen Award.

Since 1988 he has lived with his family on a small vineyard in Beavercreek, Oregon. For many years Lars Nordström worked as a technical translator in the high tech industry, but now divides his time between growing wine grapes and writing and translating literature, as well as giving talks on various Swedish-American subjects.

For an up-to-date list of Lars Nordström's publications,
please visit larsnordstrom.com